CHANGE AND
THE NEW INTERNATIONAL
ECONOMIC ORDER

TILBURG STUDIES IN ECONOMICS   20

CHANGE AND THE NEW INTERNATIONAL ECONOMIC ORDER

JAN A. VAN LITH
Editor

Tilburg School of Economics,
Social Sciences and Law
The Netherlands

Martinus Nijhoff Publishing
Boston / The Hague / London

Distributors for North America:
Martinus Nijhoff Publishing
Kluwer Boston, Inc.
160 Old Derby Street
Hingham, Massachusetts 02043

Distributors outside North America:
Kluwer Academic Publishers Group
Distribution Centre
P.O. Box 322
3300 AH Dordrecht, The Netherlands

Library of Congress Cataloging in Publication Data
Main entry under title:

Change and the new international economic order.

(Tilburg studies in economics; v. 20)
"Published under the auspices of the Department of
Economics, University of Tilburg."
1. International economic relations—Addresses,
essays, lectures. I. Lith, Jan A. van. II. Katholieke
Hogeschool. Economisch Instituut. III. Series.
HF1411.C4153   382.1   79-22888
ISBN 0-89838-028-6

Printed in the United States of America.

PREFACE

In the academic year 1977-1978 Tilburg University celebrated
its fiftieth anniversary. The commemoration involved specific
scientific activities. The theme of 'Innovation', broadly defined as 'developments in sciences and society', offered the
scientific framework in which these activities took place.
The present volume is one of the results. It consists of the
texts of a series of lectures held at the Department of Economics of Tilburg University. The Department's Colloquium
Committee, set up to organize discussions on current research,
arranged the lectures. On this occasion, the committee decided
to draw attention to the multidisciplinary character of research in the area of NIEO, the New International Economic Order. The collection of papers that eventually resulted is
published in this volume.

Gratitude is owed to the people, thanks to whom this volume
could be published: to Mr. Ad Janssen, head of the Office of
the Department of Economics for offering the secretarial facilities needed to 'process' the book, despite an understaffed
office already facing excessive work; to the 'Fifty Years Tilburg University' Committee for creating the financial ways and
means; to Mr. Jan Vingerhoets of the Development Research Institute of Tilburg University for his most valuable advice and
help; to Mr. McGivern who gave the book its final form in English. Thanks also are due to Mr. Hans Sinner, responsible for
Tilburg University Press; to Mr. van Vloten, publisher, Martinus Nijhoff, and to Mrs. Hinkenkemper, Miss Annelies Vugs and
Dr. George Embree.

Especially, gratitude is due to Miss Nanda Boers who, entirely voluntarily, offered assistance, and to Mrs. Gonny de Rooij-
Smits from the Department of Economics. Together they prepared
the camera-ready copy for the book. Their enthusiasm and efficiency helped the publication along substantially.

The book is published under the auspices of the Department
of Economics, University of Tilburg. The editor is a member of
the Department's Colloquium Committee.

Tilburg, October, 1978.

TABLE OF CONTENTS

ABOUT THE AUTHORS

1. Pieter VerLoren van Themaat,
   Professor of economic law at the University of Utrecht.

2. Gert-Jan Veerman,
   Home Office, Department of Constitutional Affairs;

   Paulien van der Ploeg,
   Legal Advisor of the Dutch Labour Party in the 'Provincia-
   le Staten'.

3. Sylvain R. Plasschaert,
   Professor at the University Faculties St. Ignatius of the
   University of Antwerp; visiting professor at the Universi-
   ty of Leuven and the College of Europe, Bruges.

4. Kurt P. Tudyka,
   Professor of political science and international relations at the Catholic University of Nijmegen.

5. Ben H. Evers,
   Director Development Research Institute, Tilburg University.

6. Antoine J. Groosman,
   Research Fellow at the Development Research Institute of
   Tilburg University.

7. Wouter Tims,
   Professor at the Free University of Amsterdam and director
   of the Centre for World Food Studies, Free University, Amsterdam.

8. Edmund P. Wellenstein,
   Former Director-General External Relations of the European
   Communities.

LIST OF ABBREVIATIONS

CIEC   CONFERENCE ON INTERNATIONAL ECONOMIC CO-OPERATION

COMECON   COUNCIL FOR MUTUAL ECONOMIC AID

DC   DEVELOPED COUNTRY

EEC   EUROPEAN ECONOMIC COMMUNITY

FAO   FOOD AND AGRICULTURAL ORGANIZATION

FDI   FOREIGN DIRECT INVESTMENT

GATT   GENERAL AGREEMENT ON TARIFFS AND TRADE

IAEA   INTERNATIONAL ATOMIC ENERGY AGENCY

IBRD   INTERNATIONAL BANK FOR RECONSTRUCTION AND DEVELOPMENT

ICFTU   INTERNATIONAL CONFEDERATION OF FREE TRADE UNIONS

IEA   INTERNATIONAL ENERGY AGENCY

IFAD   INTERNATIONAL FUND FOR AGRICULTURAL DEVELOPMENT

ILO   INTERNATIONAL LABOUR ORGANIZATION

IMF   INTERNATIONAL MONETARY FUND

LDC   LESS DEVELOPED COUNTRY

LLDC   LEAST DEVELOPED COUNTRY

MNE   MULTINATIONAL ENTERPRISE

MSA-countries = MOST SERIOUSLY AFFECTED COUNTRIES

OECD   ORGANIZATION FOR ECONOMIC CO-OPERATION AND DEVELOP-
          MENT

OEEC   ORGANIZATION FOR EUROPEAN ECONOMIC CO-OPERATION

OPEC   ORGANIZATION OF PETROLEUM EXPORTING COUNTRIES

SELA   LATIN AMERICAN ECONOMIC SYSTEM (SISTEMA ECONÓMICO
          LATINOAMERICANO)

SITC   STANDARD INTERNATIONAL TRADE CLASSIFICATION

UN   UNITED NATIONS

UNCTAD   UNITED NATIONS CONFERENCE ON TRADE AND DEVELOPMENT

UNDP UNITED NATIONS DEVELOPMENT PROGRAMME

UNEP UNITED NATIONS ENVIRONMENT PROGRAMME

UNESCO UNITED NATIONS EDUCATIONAL, SCIENTIFIC AND CULTURAL ORGANIZATION

UNIDO UNITED NATIONS INDUSTRIAL DEVELOPMENT ORGANIZATION

UNRISD UNITED NATIONS RESEARCH INSTITUTE FOR SOCIAL DEVELOPMENT

USDA UNITED STATES DEPARTMENT OF AGRICULTURE

WFC WORLD FOOD COUNCIL

WHO WORLD HEALTH ORGANIZATION

INTRODUCTION

It is a tradition in the Department of Economics of Tilburg
University to organize general discussions on current research
for the Department's entire academic staff. Thus researchers
are given the opportunity to present their research and staffmembers are enabled to exchange view on research directly or
indirectly related to their field of interest.
Within the wide range of subjects offered the general set-up
is to combine the 'supply' of current research with the 'demand' of interested Department staffmembers. The resulting
'output' is a more or less chaotic series of research discussions on completely unrelated subjects.

At the commemoration of Tilburg University's fiftieth anniversary, this tradition was slightly altered by setting a
theme for these discussions. For the jubilee year was graced
by special scientific activities within a theme chosen for the
occasion, namely 'Innovation'. The Department's general discussions on research were put within this 'scientific framework' and attention was focussed on what was broadly defined
as 'the innovative aspects of the so-called New International
Economic Order'. Within the given parameters of time, money
and indicated interests, attention was called to the multi-
dimensional character of current NIEO research. As is clearly
reflected in the composition of this volume, it was neither
the intention, nor was it possible in the given set-up, to
organize discussions in a more coherent way. An attempt made
in this volume to make a classification of the research discussed, resulted in a division into three groups of papers:
the legal aspects of the NIEO [Chapters 1 and 2]; aspects related to, broadly speaking, industry and labour [Chapters 3,
4 and 5]; commodities and agriculture in the NIEO [Chapters 6
and 7]. Chapter 8, finally, is a paper apart in the sense that
it is not only the result of research but also an analysis of
the North-South Dialogue by an important participant in the
Paris Conference.

As said, the general research discussions of the Department
of Economics are set up to present scientists and their research activities to the Department's staff. Accordingly, it
should be considered an omission not to introduce the authors
to the reader. Following is such a chapterwise introduction.

In Chapter 1 international economic law research is presented. This research focusses on the specific legal problems
with which a developing NIEO will be confronted. An important
part of the research is the attempted development of a general
theory of international economic organizations. A series of
studies has already been published by this research group,
which is composed of lawyers from the universities of Utrecht
and Leiden. In this contribution to the volume, Professor Verloren van Themaat, the project-manager and general-editor of
the research, summarizes the methods and provisional results.

Dr. Veerman, in Chapter 2, deals with economic self-determination. In his book 'Self-determination and Human Rights'
(Het Zelfbeschikkingsrecht der Naties en de Rechten van de

Mens), published in 1977, Veerman analyzed the concept of political self-determination in international law. The very personal and interesting vision developed in this book constitutes
the basis for analysis here of economic self-determination.
Together with co-author Paulien van der Ploeg, who wrote a
paper about the NIEO, he has also published a book on human
rights and law for use by members of Amnesty International
(Een Recht, Twee Averecht).

In the author's conception economic self-determination is
the pendant of the political self-determination. Starting from
article 1.2 of the Covenants on Human Rights (1966), Veerman
goes into the meaning of his concept of economic self-determination.

Professor Plasschaert did extensive research in the Third
World Center (Centrum Derde Wereld), the University Development-Research Institute in Antwerp. He is a former official
and consultant of the IBRD (the World Bank). From 1972-1977
Professor Plasschaert was Director of the Third World Center.
His main interests in development research are related to aspects of fiscal policy, the MNE and the international monetary
system. In Chapter 3 he analyses the specific tensions as
they exist in the relationship between MNE and LDC's.

Professor Tudyka, author of Chapter 4, is Chairman of the
Center of Peace Research of the Institute of Political Science
of the University of Nijmegen, and head of the Institute's
'International Relations' section. The extensive research done
at these centers, during the last years has concentrated mainly on the international activity of labour unions, especially
their policy towards MNE and related problems. In his 'Labour
Unions and the NIEO', Tudyka describes what he considers their
negative perception of international economic relations. He
outlines and comments on the labour unions' proposals for a
new policy for the developing and industrialised countries and
concludes with the role and functions labour unions see for
themselves with respect to the NIEO.

Chapter 5 is based on work done by a research group on 'Industrial Re-adjustment and the International Division of Labour'. This group is composed of researchers from the Development Research Institute of Tilburg University. Evers, the
author of Chapter 5, directs the Institute, and this research.
The aim is to analyse causes and effects of the changes taking
place in the international division of labour. The analysis
focusses on the effects for both developing and industrialised
countries, in particular with regard to trade in manufactured
products. The research is meant to provide assessment elements
for formulating a more efficient anticipatory industrial readjustment policy which takes into account the interests of
developing countries and of the Netherlands as adequately as
possible.

In his contribution in Chapter 6, Groosman analyses world
food production and trade. A description is given of past, current and expected trends and the U.N. strategy in the establishment of a NIEO is analyzed. Groosman's effort is aimed at outlining the future role of the agriculture of Third World countries in what he calls an 'international framework'. Groosman's

contribution is based on research in the field of international trade in food and agricultural requisites. The author, Research Fellow at the Tilburg Development Research Institute, has published works on the international structure and organization of the world fertilizer industry and on trade relations between developed and developing countries in the field of agricultural requisites.

Professor Tims, former Director of the Economic Analysis and Projections Department of the World Bank, is now Director of the Center for World Food Market Studies of the Free University of Amsterdam. Under his supervision a project-group on the 'World Food Problem' is conducting research into the long-term pattern of agricultural development and food supply, with emphasis on alternative national and international policy plans. In this research attention is paid to the determinants and effects of income distribution and distribution of power within the countries concerned. In Chapter 7, on 'Primary Commodities and the NIEO', Professor Tims analyses the role of primary commodities in world trade and their significance for developing countries. He discusses present policy proposals and possible alternatives on the basis of the analysis made.

Chapter 8 is the contribution of the former Director-General, External Relations, of the European Economic Communities, Dr. Wellenstein, author of the well-known report on the NIEO to the Dutch Society for International Law. Wellenstein, an insider in the EEC negotiating system, headed the negotiations on British entry into the EEC and, as EEC representative and Co-chairman of the Development Commission of CIEC, participated in the CIEC talks held in Paris between December,1975 and June, 1977. Given his insights and experience, Dr. Wellenstein was invited to elaborate on the question of whether, in his view, the North-South Dialogue was just another confrontation or a starting point for a new NIEO.

At the end of each chapter is a reference section containing a selection of works suggested by the author for further study.

1 THE CHANGING STRUCTURE OF THE INTERNATIONAL ECONOMIC LEGAL ORDER

Pieter VerLoren van Themaat

1.1. INTRODUCTION

In the years 1970 to 1972 several events of varying importance occurred which led us to consider a study on the changing structure of the international economic legal order. (2) These events were as follows:

1. In 1970 the international oil market changed from a buyer's market to a seller's market; this enabled OPEC to start its policy of price-increases which, from 1973 onwards, was bound to have an enormous impact on the international economic order.

2. In the summer of 1971 the convertibility of the dollar into gold was suspended; this event resulted in the collapse of the Bretton Woods international monetary system of fixed exchange rates.

3. Also in 1971 the Second Development Decade of the U.N. raised hopes in the developing countries of a substantial increase of transfer of incomes from the rich to the poor countries; its main architect, Professor Tinbergen, however, very soon expressed his concern that the institutional framework would prove to be insufficient for the implementation of this most important statement of policy.

4. Again in 1971, at a comparative law colloquium of the Hague Academy of International Law on regional organizations, the fact was stressed that the literature of international economic law had not yet succeeded in working out a general theory of international economic organizations. While the basic documents were fascinating, the discussion on their comparison could not fill this gap.

---

*) The reader of this chapter will find a number of technical explanations of method and content of our study in the numbered footnotes.

1

5. 1972. saw the publication of the M.I.T.study for the Club of Rome on the limits of growth which, in the Netherlands, had an immediate explosive impact on public opinion and policy-makers.

6. Also in the year 1972 President Echeverria of Mexico proposed at the third UNCTAD the working out of a Charter of Economic Rights and Duties of States.

1.2. THE NEW PROBLEMS

In 1973 a sufficient consensus seemed to exist on the ten problem   areas that should be dealt with by the international economic order in a coherent way. These problem areas were:

1. Old and new aspects of the regulation of international trade (international division of labour by the market or by planning or by a mixture of free market forces and regulation).

2. Old and new aspects of the international monetary system (monetary stability, regulation of payments and the creation, distribution and management of international liquidities).

3. A coherent policy with regard to the many aspects of the development issue. (3)

4. The supply and market regulations of energy and mineral raw materials.

5. The supply of food.

6. The limits of the possible growth of the world's population.

7. The protection of the environment.

8. The ocean regime (with the inclusion of sea-transport, sea-fishery, pollution of the oceans, the extension of jurisdiction of the coastal states and the exploitation of the ocean bed and its subsoil).

9. The control of transnational corporations and international cartels.

10. The coordination of policies with respect to all these problem areas.

1.3. METHOD OF RESEARCH

In the years 1973 and 1974, with the assistance of Professor Tinbergen, we worked out preliminary outlines of a research project on the legal changes in the existing international economic order which would be necessary in order to deal with the ten economic problems to be solved. In its final form this project would have to consist of three parts: *)

---

*) It follows from footnote (1) that the third part corresponds with chapters III, IV and V of the second part of our study and that the chapters of this summary do not correspond either with the subdivision of the second part of our study. They correspond to our most important conclusions.

1. An analysis of the tasks for the future and the historical development of international economic law from the Middle Ages up to 1974.
2. A comparative law study of the lessons to be drawn from the experience of existing international economic organizations; this comparative law study would be extended to regional and functional organizations below the world level in all parts of the world, Socialist countries and developing countries included.
3. Conclusions from a confrontation of the lessons from the existing international organizations with the lessons from the past and the tasks for the future; in 1975 we decided to add a confrontation of these conclusions with the U.N. Charter of Economic Rights and Duties of States of December 1974.

In the beginning of 1974 a grant from the Dutch Foundation of Fundamental Research enabled us to start our project with a group of fifteen international lawyers from the Universities of Leyden and Utrecht and with the assistance of Professor Tinbergen and some other economists. (At the same time Professor Tinbergen was enabled by the Club of Rome and the Dutch government to start an international economic research project on the same subject, which resulted in 1976 in the RIO report on the reshaping of the international order. (4) The approach of this latter project was very different from our own approach. It resulted in the recommendation of solutions of a more supranational character than we found to be necessary and compatible with the trends of legal development).

The first draft of the first part of our study was completed in 1975. (5) Twenty-nine specific studies of existing international economic organizations and on the legal aspects of some of the new problem areas were completed and published in 1977. They formed the basis of our comparative law research. We hope to complete our final conclusions in the course of this year. A first draft of this final part of our study is now ready.

1.4. THE HISTORICAL DEVELOPMENT OF SEVEN GENERAL STANDARDS OR PRINCIPLES OF SUBSTANTIVE LAW

A very prominent place in our study is taken by the historical development, since the twelfth century, of the seven principles or standards of substantive international economic law as summarized by Erler and Schwarzenberger.

These seven standards are:
1. the principle of reciprocity;
2. the principle of national treatment of foreigners;
3. the most-favoured-nation clause which can be found as early as 1417 in a treaty between England and Burgundy;
4. the principle of the open door;
5. preferential systems in favour of forms of closer cooperation with specific countries or categories of countries;
6. a principle of equity;
7. a minimum standard.

It is interesting to note that, with the exception of the ob-
solete principle of the open door, (6) all of these very old
principles or standards are still very relevant. All of them
can still be found in the Charter of Economic Rights and Duties of States. And all of them play an important role in many existing international economic organizations.

This, however, does not exclude the fact that important
new developments of these general principles of substantive
law have taken place since the Second World War.

In the most developed international economic organizations
like the EEC, the principle of reciprocity was replaced by a
principle of equal rights of all member states towards the
organization itself. This development has very important legal consequences, as the Community Court of Justice has made
clear. (7)

Again, in the most developed international economic organizations of states with a market economy or a mixed economy,
the principle of national treatment of foreigners was extended to cover foreign goods, foreign services and foreign capital by the establishment of a general principle of non-dis-
crimination on grounds of nationality. Moreover in the EEC the
principle became self-executing. (8)

The most-favoured-nation clause developed from parallel
clauses in bilateral treaties to an international standard,
applied by GATT and leading to multilateral trade negotiations
instead of bilateral negotiations.

The old preferential standard led to the establishment of
customs unions, free trade areas, a general preferential system and other preferential regimes under the supervision of
GATT. These new forms of preferential regimes partly applied
to groups of countries with particularly strong common economic interests.Partly they were admitted in favour of developing countries in order to compensate the inherent weakness
of these countries (positive discrimination).

The old principle of equity also plays an important role
in many international economic organizations and the same is
true with regard to a minimum standard in various forms. More
fundamental, however, are three new developments.

Many of the age-old principles can be summarized as various
forms of a principle of equality. For example, the principles
of reciprocity, of national treatment and of the most-favoured-nation clause can be largely summarized as principles of
formal equality. All foreign states and all foreigners have
to be treated in the same way. This formal principle of non-
discrimination, still dear to the U.S.A., has been built upon
however by various forms of a substantive equality principle.
This means various things, but the general idea is: if situations are substantially different, the principle of equality
itself requires that these situations be dealt with in different ways in proportion to these differences. As one example,
the great differences in economic importance of states led to
different voting rights in regard to the function of the GNP
or other criteria in a number of important organizations. The
very different levels of import duties require that higher tariffs be reduced more than lower tariffs. Furthermore, a prin-

ciple of national treatment of foreigners is no longer sufficient to provide equal opportunities in international competition; it should be fleshed out by measures of harmonization
of legal and financial conditions of international competition
established by the various states for enterprises working
within their territory. Finally, the basic concepts of the
World Bank and of the regional and social policies within states, within the European Communities and within other regional
and international organizations all express the idea that weaker groups in society should be treated in a preferential way
in order to compensate their weaker position. Formal equality
develops to substantive justice, based on substantive equal
rights and aiming at greater substantive equality. Because
this new concept worked towards a new basic legal value within
and between the Western countries, Western countries should
not refuse its application in their relations to the developing countries. (9)

A second new development can be found in the various forms
of a new standard of international economic relations: the
principle of solidarity, the logical consequence of the growing economic interdependence of states. Our analysis of existing organizations brought to light three main forms of this
new standard:
1. obligations for member countries to take into account the
   international external effects of their national economic
   policy;
2. bilateral and multilateral forms of financial, technical
   and legal assistance of states confronted with temporary
   or more structural difficulties in the implementation of
   their justified economic goals;
3. obligations of international cooperation within the framework of international economic organizations. 10)

A third important new development is to be found in the
fact that the factual presumption of a principle of freedom
for states and of international economic transactions which
underlies the old standards has been upgraded to a legal principle of sovereign equality of states and, in some of the most
developed international economic organizations in self-executing international rights and duties of enterprises and other
non-governmental actors in international economic relations.
In the EEC these rights and duties of private and other non-
governmental actors have to be upheld by the national courts
under the supervision of the European Communities Court of
Justice. (11)

1.5. TOWARDS A GENERAL THEORY OF INTERNATIONAL ECONOMIC ORGA-
ZATIONS

It is the new principle of international solidarity which
brings me to discuss very briefly our analysis of the most
important existing international economic organizations. Of
course this analysis of about 1500 pages cannot be really
summarized within five minutes of reading time, but some of
our most interesting findings can be highlighted.

First of all we found a very clear correlation between the degree of development, the structure of production, the economic
system and the political system of member states of an international organization and the institutional set-up, substantive legal principles, legal powers and policy-instruments of
the organizations themselves. This indeed easily explains why,
for example, the (East European) Council of Mutual Economic Assistance is not and will never be a supranational organization
with important powers of its own (12) and why the age-old-
standards summarized by Schwarzenberger have no great relevance for socialist integration as long as Socialist states
maintain a system of central planning of input, output and investments of enterprises. (13) Socialist integration must for
fundamental reasons be based on intergovernmental cooperation
and not on transfer of sovereign rights to international institutions. On the other hand a growing interdependence of
states with a market economy or a mixed economy favours the
development of international organizations with independent
institutions, having supranational powers. The greater the
interdependence, the greater the possibility of transfer of
powers. Because international monetary interdependence is
greater than international interdependence in trade, the powers of IMF are greater than those of GATT. And because the
trade-interdependence of the West-European countries between
themselves is very much greater than their interdependence
with the rest of the world, the powers of the EEC-institutions
are also greater than those of GATT. (14) Perhaps our most interesting conclusion, however, is that both intergovernmental
and more supranational international economic organizations
are using instruments for the implementation of their goals
which belong to two or more of the following four categories
of:
1. exchange of information,
2. procedures of consultation,
3. unconditional and conditional financial incentives and
4. binding rules, regulations, directives and other forms of
   binding decisions.

On two aspects of the fourth category of instruments, however, there is a fundamental difference between organizations
of states with a mixed economy and states with centrally-
planned economies.
   In the first place permanent basic principles of equality
and self-executing rights and duties of citizens can only be
found in organizations of states with a mixed economy. The
age-old-standards indeed are closely connected to the role of
the market in international relations.
   In the second place binding supranational regulations and
decisions in order to correct or to replace the market-mechanism prove to be possible only in organizations of states
with a mixed economy or on relatively minor points which cannot be regulated at all effectively by separate states. (15)
In the case of Socialist integration and also in the case of
the OPEC one therefore finds complicated combinations of non-
binding resolutions and binding national measures or inter-

state contracts for the implementation of these resolutions.
The experience of the EEC and of the Andean Group, however,
seems to indicate that, between states with a mixed economy,
supranational binding coordination of overall economic policies, or of very essential parts of national economic policy
is not possible either. (16) The experience of the COMECON
and of the Andean Group therefore seems also relevant for the
adaptation of the international economic order to new needs.
We should not forget indeed that the larger part of the above-
mentioned ten problem areas of the future cannot be solved
by the market mechanism alone. Nor that some of these problem
areas stem from essential parts of national economic policy,
with no state willing to transfer its sovereignty to international institutions taking majority-decisions or other decisions on which the member states of international institutions have no decisive influence.

1.6. TOWARDS A NEW GENERAL THEORY OF INTERNATIONAL ECONOMIC
     LAW

Initially we thought that our research would lead to the addition of a general theory on international economic organizations as a separate chapter in the existing general theory
of international economic public law; in fact the bulky chapter of the final part of our study contains an effort to develop such a theory. Nevertheless our initial assumption finally proved to be incorrect. On the contrary, it proved to
be rather easier and far more satisfactory to integrate the
general theory of international economic organizations into
the existing general theory of international economic law.
Such a general theory should then have the following chapters, the sequence of which indicates at the same time the
line of the explanation of the trends of development.

1. Points of departure: the existence of sovereign states
   with different structures of production, different degrees
   of development and different economic, social and political systems; the different degrees of freedom of decision-
   making on international economic transactions for enterprises and citizens and the degree of recognition of
   rights and duties of enterprises and citizens in this respect; the degree of economic interdependence of states.
   Such differences in points of departure largely explain
   the differences between regional organizations and part of
   the set-up of worldwide organizations as well.

2. General and specific objectives to be realized by international economic law and the scope ratione materiae of the
   various parts of international economic law. (17)

3. The substantive basic law principles or standards of freedom, equality and solidarity (for states and their subjects) and the general principles for their implementation. (18)

4. The substantive law steering-instruments for attaining the general and specific objectives of international economic law (as far as the market-mechanism is deemed to be insufficient in this respect). (19)

5. The scope ratione personae and ratione territoriae and the institutional set-up of international economic organizations necessary for attaining the general and specific objectives of international economic law. (20)

6. The solution of conflicts between international economic organizations (the important problem of effective coordination of their activities, insofar as the market is unble to provide this coordination).

7. The solution of conflicts in other relations regulated by international economic law (between organizations and their member states or citizens, between states, between states and citizens or between citizens).

1.7. THE DEFICIENCIES OF BOTH THE EXISTING INTERNATIONAL ECONOMIC ORDER AND OF THE CHARTER OF ECONOMIC RIGHTS AND DUTIES OF STATES

This framework of a general theory served then as a system of reference for our analysis of the legal deficiencies of the existing international economic order in view of the new objectives, for our analysis of the Charter of Economic Rights and Duties of States and for our conclusions with regard to possible improvements.

Our analysis of the existing system of international economic organizations led us to the conclusion that in all chapters of the system of reference further developments are necessary. More important in this respect, however, is our conclusion that the necessary further developments are nothing else than further developments of existing trends in positive law as indicated earlier. Moreover, for the greater part these necessary improvements seem to be compatible with the basic legal values of Western states and Socialist states and they seem to serve the interests of developing countries as well. What is necessary however is the willingness of the Western world to also apply its basic legal values in its relationship to developing countries. (21) Curiously enough, the shortcomings of the U.N. Charter of Economic Rights and Duties of States seem to be far more disastrous for the developing countries and the world as a whole than the shortcomings of the existing international order. To avoid misunderstandings in this respect, I immediately add that I sympathize with the Charter in a general way. I do not think, moreover, that from the point of view of basic legal values of the Western world most of the criticism of the Charter is well founded. This applies to its article 2 on nationalization, because in Western countries the legal system of property rights is also being considered as primarily a matter of national law with a possibility of international conventions in this respect, a possibility which is left open also in the Charter. It applies also to the raw materials issue, because in this respect the Charter only applies to all raw materials what the Western countries are doing themselves with regard to agriculture. It finally applies to the famous principle of price-indexation of export prices in article 28. If, from a practical point of view, I share the doubts about whether this principle can be made workable, from a fundamental point of view this principle is just another application of an indexation principle which originated in the Western World itself. From a more general point of view it results from article 14 of the Charter that it is not true that the Charter, in a more general way, wants to substitute planning for the market. On the contrary, the Charter seems quite compatible with a community of states with a mixed system of competition _and_ state interventions.

Our criticism concerns other general and specific aspects of the Charter. From a general point of view it shows surprising gaps, a lack of system and internal contradictions. (22) From a more specific point of view, its shortcomings in regard to elements in the various chapters of our system of reference are far greater than in regard to those of the existing system of international organizations.

To start with the scope of the Charter ratione personae, we conclude that no grip on the reality of a mixed international economic order will be possible if the Charter does not also provide for rights and duties of transnational corporations. Effective control of transnational corporations and international cartels can only be achieved by such an extension of the scope ratione personae of the Charter. Moreover the fundamental aims of a new international economic order to achieve a life of dignity and well-being for all world citizens will never be attained if the Charter does not provide for certain fundamental rights of all citizens in this respect as already developed in earlier resolutions of the U.N.. (23) In the third place, if the point of departure of sovereign states is certainly justified, the Charter should explicitly recognize that the use of sovereign rights can be limited by international law just as the use of property rights can be limited by national law. Moreover the Charter should recognize that functional sovereignty on specific subjects can be transferred to international organizations. On all these points the Charter remains behind the actual state of development of international economic law.

Considering the categlogue of objectives of a new international economic order one is struck by the fact that the Charter does not mention any objectives with regard to the international monetary order. Nor with regard to the supply of energy and food. Nor with regard to the population issue. Nor with regard to the many other aspects of the ocean domain than the exploitation of the sea-bad and ocean floor and the subsoil thereof. Nor with regard to the international control of transnational corporations and international cartels. Nor with regard to the overall task of providing for an effective system of coordination of various new ac-

tivities in order to assure their consistency. A Charter of
Economic Rights and Duties of States should contain a short,
but complete catalogue of the objectives to be attained, with
a possibility of later amendments. The legal principles, instruments and institutions have to be adapted to these objectives. In fact the majority of the objectives of a new international economic order recognized by the U.N. at other occa-
sions has not been mentioned in the Charter. Coordination
with the Declaration and Program of Action of May 1974 apparently has been quite insufficient.

With regard to the elaboration of the principles of freedom we concluded that the provisions in the first chapter and
in Charter articles 1, 7, 16, 26 and 32 on various aspects of
the principle of sovereignty should, for systematic reasons,
be brought together and completed as indicated. Moreover the
possibility of enforceable economic rights of citizens to
participate in international economic intercourse should be
recognized in the Charter. Finally we pleaded in favour of a
general duty of states to meet basic needs of their citizens,
as far as necessary with the support of international organizations. (24) Doubt was expressed if, without such a duty, a
readiness of rich countries to contribute to raising the living standards of poor countries could reasonably be expected. (25)

With regard to the equality principle in its new forms, we
concluded that the Charter remained somewhat behind the present state of international economic law except on the point
of preferential regimes in favour of developing countries.

With regard to the various forms of the new principle of
solidarity, the Charter mentions, in a rather vague way,
forms of financial and technical assistance and duties to co-
operate. One cannot say, however, that in these respects the
Charter proffers important innovations with regard to the
actual state of development of international law. Even a
clear principle that cooperation should be organized in such
a way that all the objectives and basic principles of the
Charter can be realized is lacking. The Charter, moreover, in
comparison to existing international law, is particularly
weak with regard to the basic idea that the principle of sovereignty should logically include a principle of responsibility by which states avoid harmful external effects of their
economic policies. Our study indicates how such a principle
could be implemented if one looks at existing solutions of
this fundamental appendix to every principle of freedom in an
interdependent society.

Finally we found that the Charter contains hardly any
principles with regard to the steering instruments and the
institutional set-up necessary for attaining the new objectives. Nor does it contain any clear provisions for the resolution of conflicts. The first two of these last gaps are
particularly surprising because the entire Charter is based
on the idea that the market mechanism alone is not sufficient
to attain the basic objectives of a more just international
economic order.

The existing international economic order is certainly

based mainly on the market mechanism. The Western world should also easily recognize, however, that this is no longer the whole truth with regard to their internal economic policy. State interventions in the economy are many in all countries of the world. As soon as this fact of the mixed character of the national economic systems is recognized, it follows from one of our basic conclusions that the international order has to follow. It also has to take on the character of a mixed international economic system. Next to the market, the coordination of national interventions in the economy will then have to find its place in the international economic order. (26) It is not at all clear that this inevitable conclusion is recognized by the Charter in a more general way.

The Charter's lack of resolutions to conflicts is also surprising because the whole experience of the existing national and international economic order shows that satisfactory procedures for the resolution of conflicts are particularly important for the weak, in this case for the developing states in their relation to strong states and strong transnational corporations. And, as everywhere in the world, also for weak citizens in their relationship to the state, to strong corporations and to strong international organizations.

Our final conclusion with regard to the Charter is, therefore, that it needs substantial amendments, not only from the point of view of the developing countries but also from the point of view of all other countries in the world. It seems clear indeed that the international economic order as it stands is no longer sufficiently adaptable to cope with the basic problems of the Western countries themselves. It is no better adapted to deal with new Western problems than it is to deal with the needs of the developing countries or with the problems raised by the coexistence of state-trading-countries and countries with a mixed economy. Therefore, in my opinion, it is to be regretted that the Western world up to now has not been able to formulate a consistent and constructive counterproposal to the U.N. Charter of Economic Rights and Duties of States.

According to our comparative law findings, such a counterproposal should be worked out on the following basis:

1. Points of departure: the existence of sovereign states and the necessity in an interdependent world to regulate the use of sovereign rights as far as necessary for the implementation of common objectives; recognition of national jurisdiction with regard to property law; the possibility of recognition by international economic organizations of self-executing rights and duties of enterprises and citizens with regard to activities of international legal relevance.

2. A list of general and specific objectives to be achieved on the world level, with periodical amendments.

3. Substantive basic principles of freedom, equality and solidarity of states and their subjects, and general principles for their implementation.

4. A provision stipulating that the charter of every international economic organization has to indicate which steering instruments can be used for attaining its more inter-
   ventionist objectives.

5. General institutional principles with regard to international economic organizations and the relations between
   worldwide and regional organizations.

6. Rules for the resolution of conflicts between international organizations.

7. Rules for the resolution of conflicts between international organizations and their member states or their citizens, between member states, between member states and citizens and between non-governmental actors in international economic relations - as far as these conflicts are related to the activities of international organizations
   (the notion of "citizens" is to be understood here in a
   wide sense, including all non-governmental actors).

8. Rules for the periodical amendment of the Charter as indicated in article 34 of the Charter.

With regard to the legal character of the Charter our study
concludes that it is too early for codification of a charter
in the form of an enforceable treaty, but that a certain normative effect of the Charter cannot be denied. More generally
one is struck by the fact that in German literature, where
the concept of an economic constitution has been primarily
developed, the idea of a binding force of economic constitutions in general has been rejected for more fundamental reasons. (27) Such a binding force would be incompatible with
the open character and the necessary adaptability of an economic constitution to changing economic situations and ideo-
logies. If the Charter has to be considered as an international economic constitution, it therefore should not be assimi-
lated into a constitution in the traditional sense of the
word. Codification would hamper, not promote, progress.

1.8. OUTLINE OF A NEW PATTERN OF INTERNATIONAL ECONOMIC ORGA-
     NIZATIONS

An important conclusion of our study is that the basic characteristics of the international economic order are very
largely a function of economic and technological developments
and not of a free choice by governments. This conclusion certainly does not exclude keeping certain options open. Within
rather narrow margins one is free, for example, to put a heavier accent on the freedom principle or on the solidarity
principle. One can reject certain forms of the equality principle and within narrow margins one can also choose for more
supranational or for more intergovernmental structures of international organizations. Our study gives some indications
on such possible options.
   With regard to the scope of worldwide economic organiza-

tions such small margins of change in the existing pattern also exist. However, in order to deal with the ten central problem areas in a new economic world order on which consensus seems to exist, ten organizations or groups of organizations seem to be necessary on the world level:

1. Taking GATT and UNCTAD as a point of departure, a new International Trade Organization should deal with the liberalization and regulation of international trade (non-tariff obstacles included), the general principles for the regulation of the markets of raw materials and energy, and the control of international cartels.

2. The IMF should remain responsible for the international monetary system and the solution of the many new problems in this field.

3. While GATT, IMF and the U.N. themselves certainly have their important roles to play in an international redistribution of wealth, a more active policy of planning of development should be concentrated around the World Bank Group and regional development banks. This does not mean that the ILO, FAO, UNESCO and WHO organizations should no longer also deal with problems of employment and basic needs in the developing countries. It is the World Bank Group, however, which - together with regional development banks - should continue to implement general and specific development projects with financial support and technical assistance. Its means to assist poor countries and poor parts of the population of developing countries should be strengthened (basic-needs strategy).

4. The International Atomic Energy Agency of the U.N. should be restructured into an International Agency for the development of all new sources of energy and for the promotion of more efficiency in the use of energy.

5. Technical assistance in the management of the growth of populations (family-planning) should continue to be provided by the WHO.

6. UNEP should remain the coordinating agency for the protection of the environment.

7. The supply of food should remain the concern of the FAO.

8. A coordinating organization with regard to all aspects of the ocean domain seems inevitable.

9. A specific institution of the U.N. itself should be entrusted with the control of transnational corporations, because of the multiple aspects of this phenomenon.

10. The United Nations Economic and Social Council (with a new director general appointed to this effect) should also be entrusted with the very important task of effective coordination of all the abovementioned activities within the framework of an indicative world plan which guarantees the reciprocal compatibility of the various activities with special regard to the multiple aspects of

the development issue. It is clear that this task raises
very difficult institutional and political problems, but
it is necessary.

1.9. CONCLUDING REMARKS

Apart from worldwide economic organizations, regional economic organizations should continue to increase in number and
importance. While our study contains a number of indications
in this respect, it would lead us too far from our main object to discuss these indications in this summary. (28) In a
general way one can conclude from our study that, with some
exceptions on both sides, regional organizations are more
effective than worldwide organizations in the implementation
of their tasks. Their limited territorial scope, however,
means that worldwide economic organizations will be ever
more necessary to deal with problems which are problems for
the world as a whole.

FOOTNOTES

1. In fact this paper presents a summary of some of the conclusions of a first draft of the second and concluding
   part of our study. We hope to complete this second part in
   the course of 1978. This second part will have five chapters: (I) The substantive problems of international economic law and the state of this new branch of international
   law at the start of our research project in early 1974;
   (II) The existing system of international economic organizations; (III) Shortcomings of the existing system and legal principles for their resolution; (IV) Analysis of the
   U.N. Charter of Economic Rights and Duties of States; (V)
   Summary and final conclusions.
   The most voluminous Chapter II, like Chapters I and IV, is
   purely analytical in character. It is based on 29 specific
   analytical studies of existing international economic organizations and related problem areas of international economic law on which more details are given in footnote (5).
   Its purpose is to give an analytical foundation for further development of the existing general theory of international economic law, as analysed in Chapter I. Chapter III,
   after giving the framework of such a new general theory,
   briefly examines the possibilities to use such a framework
   for finding solutions for difficulties with which the existing organizations actually find themselves confronted.
   Chapter IV, on the other hand, examines the possibilities
   of constructive critical conclusions with regard to the
   Charter of Economic Rights and Duties of States, based on
   the components of such a general theory. Chapter V summarizes the main findings in the previous chapters of our
   study and draws some final conclusions with an indication
   of alternative solutions for the most fundamental legal issues.
   The study thus is mainly an analytical study. It is not a
   plea for a new international economic order as asked by the
   developing countries, but mainly an analysis of the historical development and present state of international economic law and an effort to contribute to the development of a
   consistent general legal theory for their explanation.
   While the existence of a number of new problem areas is as-
   sumed, the way in which problems should be solved is not;
   this is what a new international economic order would be
   concerned with.
   The fact that we do not assume a priori the need of a new
   international economic order leads us to come to rather
   severe but, we hope, constructive criticism of the Charter
   of Economic Rights and Duties of States. Nevertheless our
   analysis of the trends of development of international
   economic law since the Middle Ages and our analysis of the
   difficulties met by existing organizations indicate the
   likelihood of the need of new fundamental changes in the
   existing international economic order. If our basic as-

sumptions in Chapter I on the existence of new problem
areas are right, the analysis of the legal principles for
their solution in Chapter III increases this likelihood.
We feel that, finally therefore, our analysis of trends of
change, undertaken independently of the great call of developing countries for a new international economic order,
may constitute lawyer's modest contribution to narrowing
the gap between the concepts of the "three worlds" with
regard to the future of our international economic order.
While we feel that the framework of a general theory,
which is the main result of our study, facilitates the
search for new solutions, it certainly leaves room for alternative solutions; some of these alternative solutions
will be indicated in the final chapter of our study. Most
of their components, however, have not been included in
this summary because of their provisional character.

2. The study has been undertaken by a group of fifteen international lawyers from the Universities of Utrecht and Leyden, most of whom have had considerable practical or research experience with many of the problems we studied.
Moreover we got valuable information and advice from other
lawyers familiar with the practice of organizations like
GATT, IMF, the World Bank, COMECON and OPEC. Finally with
regard to the economic aspects, we were assisted by Prof.
Dr. Jan Tinbergen and some other able economists. In April
and May of 1978, I had the opportunity to discuss the provisional conclusions of this paper with members of the legal staff of the United Nations and a number of specific
questions with members of the legal staffs of the IMF and
the World Bank and with other experts in the United States.
These discussions will lead to a number of clarifications
and corrections in the final draft of the second part of
our study, the outline of which has been given in footnote
(1). Some of these clarifications will be indicated in
other footnotes.

3. From a legal point of view, the most important of these
aspects can be summarized as
   a. problems of a just allocation of power (the problem of
      the voting rights of developing countries in interna-
      tional organizations and other institutional problems
      with regard to the international decision-making pro-
      cess, as well as the clarification of the concept of
      state sovereignty and the rights and duties of states in
      relations to other states, foreign corporations, their
      own subjects, etc.);
   b. a more just geographical distribution of income (by
      trade and international regulation of trade conditions,
      by an equitable allocation of international financial
      liquidities (S.D.R.'s), adjusted to the development-tar-
      gets and by other forms of transfer of financial resources;
   c. a more just distribution of know-how in the widest sence
      (the much discussed problem of transfer of technology
      being a relatively minor part of this third aspect).

It has to be stressed, that neither in this problem area, nor in any other problem area does the list imply any specific solution to the problems concerned. The list only implies consensus on the existence of the problems. With regard to their solution, opinions in 1973 were and still are very divided. To illustrate this with regard to the development issue: with regard to voting rights in existing organizations, for example, many experts feel that not much more is necessary than adaptation of existing systems to new economic facts in accordance with the existing criteria. With regard to the distribution of incomes, many experts feel that a more effective liberalization of international trade and an international monetary system based on sound and rather orthodox monetary concepts would solve most of the problems far better than any conceivable increase of aid or other artificial forms of transfer of financial resources. With regard to transfer of technology, even many experts of developing countries feel that this is a wrong issue and that developing countries on the contrary should develop their own technology, adapted to their needs.

4. Jan Tinbergen, coordinator, Reshaping the international order, a report to the Club of Rome, New York 1976.

5. Published in Dutch by T.M.C. Asser Instituut, H.D.Tjeenk Willink and A.W.Sijthoff in 1977. It consists of the five following volumes:
   Volume I.1   A study of P.J.G.Kapteyn on The United Nations and the international economic order
   Volume I.2   Organisations and problems in international trade
                1. D.C.Meerburg, The GATT
                2. P.J.Slot, Technical obstacles to trade
                3. W.H.Vermeulen, Agreements on raw materials
                4. P.VerLoren van Themaat, The OPEC
                5. R.Barents, The International Energy Agency
                6. T.P.J.N.van Rijn, International cartels
                7. T.P.J.N.van Rijn, Multinational enterprises
   Volume I.3   Organisations in the international monetary field and organisations for financing development
                1. R.Barents, Introduction to the studies on international monetary organizations
                2. R.Barents, The International Monetary Fund
                3. R.Barents, Regional monetary cooperation in Western Europe
                4. R.Barents, Financial Support Fund of the OECD
                5. R.Barents, The Bank for International Settlements
                6. P.J.G.Kapteyn, Introduction to the studies on international organizations for financing development
                7. R.Barents, The World Bank

All the studies of specific international organizations
are based on a uniform scheme of analysis which, in summary, covers the following subjects:
1. The objectives of the organization, their development
   in the course of time and their relations to the objectives of other organizations.
2. The scope of the organization (ratione personae, ratione
   materiae and ratione temporis).
3. Institutional characteristics (including decision-making procedures and budgetary provisions).
4. Substantive law characteristics (exchange of information, procedures of consultation and non-binding recommendations, financial incentives to follow certain policies and binding substantive rules as policy-instruments; procedures to resolve conflicts; analysis of the
   development of policy instruments in the course of
   time).

6. This principle in fact was mainly applied with regard to
   colonial or other dependant states.

7. One of the consequences is that member states are not allowed not to respect certain treaty provisions because
   other member states did not respect them either or because
   the European Community did not yet find an appropriate solution for an economic problem which led them to take unilateral action in violation of treaty provisions. See, for
   example, cases 2 and 3/62 (Commission vs Luxemburg and
   Belgium) and case 78/76 (Steineke vs Federal Republic of
   Germany) in the collections of Jurisprudence of the Court
   of Justice of the European Communities, published by the
   Court.

8. This implies that private persons can invoke the principle before a national court against the state concerned.
   See, for many examples: Kapteyn-VerLoren van Themaat, Introduction to the law of the European Communities, Lon-
   don-Deventer-Alphen aan de Rijn 1973, Chapters III and
   VII.

9. From the authors from developing countries who argue in
   the same sense I mention M.Manley, Parallels of equity.
   New horizons in economic cooperation, Round Table 1975,
   335-347 and J.S.Ramphal, The other world in this one: the
   promise of the new international economic order, Round
   Table 1976, 61-72.

10. See, for good examples of all three forms, articles 5, 6,
    103, par.1, 107, par.1 and 108 par.2 of the EEC Treaty;
    for the second form, see particularly IMF, World Bank
    Group and UNDP; for the third form, COMECON, OEEC/OECD
    and OPEC.

11. See Kapteyn-VerLoren van Themaat, op.cit. (footnote (8)),
    Chapter VI. It should be stressed here that EEC experien-
    ce seems to prove that the recognition of self-executing
    international rights and duties of enterprises is also a
    precondition for effective control of transnational cor-
    porations and international cartels. There is no example
    that intergovernmental cooperation has ever led to as ef-
    fective control of international cartels and misbehaviour
    of transnational corporations as the control exercised
    under the EEC treaty. The reason is that for purely legal
    reasons alone, individual states have no effective grip
    on such transnational phenomena. Because they are unable
    to establish facts outside their territory and to enforce
    decisions outside their territory, even international
    obligations for states to act against such phenomena can-
    not remove this ineffectiveness of national control. Even
    a powerful state like the United States is confronted re-
    gularly with the territorial limits of its power to con-
    trol effectively the harmful internal effects of actions
    of transnational corporations and international cartels
    outside its territory. The struggle of developing coun-
    tries to win recognition of their right to control trans-
    national corporations therefore seems to be bound to lead
    to disillusion.

12. See our study of the COMECON in Volume I.4.4 of the first
    part of our study (see footnote (5)).

13. If the state itself is responsible and takes the economic
    and financial risks for such decisions, this means in
    fact: (1) that it also has to be owner of the means of
    production; (2) that it cannot accept supranational deci-
    sions on the points mentioned as long as a supranational
    organization does not also take over the economic and fi-
    nancial risks of wrong decisions; (3) that it makes no

sense to adopt the age-old seven standards of Schwarzenberger because these standards are based on the presumption of free decisions of enterprises with regard to investments, production and marketing (restricted certainly, but not excluded, by state regulation).

14. See Volumes I.2.1, I.3.2 and I.4.4 of our project (cf.
footnote 5).

15. See our studies on raw material agreements, European
Communities and regional organizations of developing
countries, mentioned in footnote (5).

16. See Volumes I.4.4 and I.4.6 of our study, mentioned in
footnote (5). The explanation of this fact is to be
found in the circumstance that no country can accept to
bear the political, economic, social and financial risks
of wrong supranational decisions ·on essential parts of
economic policy as long as there is no supranational
parliamentary control of such decisions or at least a
financial responsibility of the supranational organization for the economic and financial consequences of such
decisions. The common agricultural policy of the EEC
seems to indicate that as soon as such a financial responsibility is accepted, transfer of powers to the supranational level becomes a real option. Even there,
however, the fact that national ministers of agriculture
may be confronted with the political consequences of decisions made in Brussels (by not being re-elected at the
next national elections) has had the consequence that no
member state easily accepts being overruled by a majority vote on vital issues.

17. When speaking of objectives I think of qualitative and
quantitative objectives with regard to growth, employment, international division of labour, regional disparities of income, monetary stability, supply and demand
of scarce resources, protection of the environment, etc..
When speaking of the scope ratione materiae I think of a
rational division of general and specific problem areas,
as mentioned in paragraph 1.2 of this summary, between
the various international organizations. See also paragraph 1.8.

18. Organizations like COMECON, raw material agreements,
OPEC, the International Energy Agency of the OECD, the
World Bank, UNDP and various international funds will
put a main accent on principles of solidarity. An organization like GATT will put it on principles of freedom
and equality for the various economic actors. In most of
the other organizations we found a combination of the
three categories of principles. In a very general way
the equality principles then serve to support standards
of freedom of states and/or private economic actors,
principles of solidarity support both principles of

freedom (self-reliance) and principles of substantive
equality.

19. Particularly important for all the organizations we analysed is the exchange of information. Further development of this instrument can also improve the effectiveness of national policies with regard to many of the
transnational problem areas mentioned in paragraph 1.2 of
this summary. The effectiveness and international compatibility and mutual support of national policies can be
increased further by effective consultation and mutual
assistance procedures. Financial incentives and technical assistance can contribute to attain common goals as
mentioned in footnote (17). Common binding decisions, be
they in a more supranational form or in the intergovernmental forms of classical international treaties and
other agreements, are indicated with regard to problem
areas like market regulations for raw materials, the
protection of the environment, the ocean domain and the
control of transnational corporations and international
cartels. With regard to the protection of the environment and the control of transnational corporations and
international cartels outside national jurisdiction,
such international binding instruments should also be
binding for private economic actors for the reasons mentioned in footnote (11). General principles of freedom
and equality for economic actors are also based mainly
on binding international treaties.

20. It results from our specific studies, mentioned in footnote (5), that the institutional set-up is partly influenced by the points of departure, mentioned under (1),
then by the general and specific objectives of the organization concerned, by the substantive basic law principles and by the substantive law steering instruments for
attaining the objectives of the organization. This explains why the variety of solutions and possible improvements we found in the institutional field is so great
and must be so great.

21. This does certainly not mean that the Western world
should try to impose its basic national legal values on
non-economic issues like parliamentary democracy or human rights on the rest of the world (see P.VerLoren van
Themaat, "Some basic legal issues of a new international
economic order: a western point of view", Netherlands
International Law Review, Volume XXIV (1977), pp.523-524.
As far as developing countries are willing to accept
such basic tenets of our Western international economic
system as the standards of freedom and equality or the
principles of solidarity, implemented by the common
agricultural policy as developed by the EEC, the belief
in our own basic legal values should lead us to accept
their demands, based on these same legal values, substantive equality standards included. From a realistic

point of view it should then be kept in mind, however,
that as there is a difference in degree between the application of substantive equality standards within national territories and its application within the European
Communities (more equality and collective economic and
social security within member states than between member
states), it cannot be expected that the degree of substantive equality in, let us say, incomes per capita between
the Common Market and developing countries will ever
reach the same degree (1:3) as between Common Market
countries. We found indeed that growing international solidarity is apparently a function of the growing interdependence of states. The interdependence between the peoples of regional organizations is generally smaller than
their interdependence on the national level, but greater
than their interdependence with the rest of the world. In
the same way, their regional solidarity and willingness
to apply standards of substantive equality normally will
be greater on the regional level than on the world level.
This conclusion seems particularly important with regard
to the income gaps between countries. In real life, international solidarity is a function of the degree of international economic interdependence and mutual economic
interests. If the disparity of per capita incomes between
the Western countries and the developing countries could
be reduced within the next two or three decades to 10:1
this therefore would already be an enormous success. At
the same time the disparity of incomes within developing
countries between the richest 20 percent and the poorest
20 percent of the population should then be reduced to
less than 10:1. The country-reports of the World Bank
show that such a goal is still far from being reached in
many of the developing countries and this fact affects
the willingness of the Western World to reduce the income
gap between per capita incomes in their countries and the
developing countries. See also on this issue Chapters 6
and 10 of the RIO report (footnote (4)).

22. The Declaration and the Program of Action on the new international economic order of May 1974 are much better in
some of these respects, but obviously the time necessary
for adaptation of the Charter to these instruments was
insufficient. The nature of these other instruments, on
the other hand, implies that they do not indicate efficient legal solutions for the problems mentioned. It
would not be fair, therefore, to also apply the test of
confrontation with the outline of a general theory of international economic law to these instruments.

23. E.g. art.25 and 28 of the Universal Declaration on Human
Rights, A/Res 1217 (III): "a standard of living adequate
for the health and well-being, including food, clothing,
housing and medical care and necessary social services"
in "a social and international order" in which this
right "can be fully realized". Cf. Ige F.Dekker, "The

new international economic order and the legal relevance of structural violence", Revue Belge de Droit International, 1976, p.498.

24. The policy of the World Bank Group also seems to go in this direction.

25. During his election campaign President Carter made the remark that Americans are no longer willing to tax the poor in the rich countries in order to support the rich in the poor countries (quoted by R.N.Cooper, "A New International Economic Order for Mutual Gain", Foreign Policy, 1977, pp.66-120).

26. This seems indeed one of the lessons to be drawn from the crises of such international organizations as EEC, IMF and GATT.

27. G.Rinck, Wirtschaftsrecht, fourth edition (1974), remarks that the notion of an economic constitution includes the basic decisions on limitation, orientation or freedom of the economic process, especially on such points as free exercise of economic activities, market regulation, competition and ownership of means of production. One could add the basic decisions on distribution of incomes and economic power. Essential in this definition is that while these basic decisions have an overriding normative value with regard to specific economic laws, they are not codified within the Constitution in the strict sense of the word because this would deprive them of the necessary flexibility. Their quasi-constitutional character stems from the fact that they cannot be neglected without endangering the consistency of the economic system as a whole. In the same way, an international economic constitution, without being legally enforceable, should indicate those basic principles which can assure the consistency of the international economic system and which therefore should be respected by all of the more specific regulations and policies.

28. Our study of a number of regional organizations of developing countries made clear that their weakness can be explained partly by the weakness of economic structures, political regimes and administrations of the cooperating countries, partly by conflicts of interests and policies and partly by insufficient economic interdependence of the countries concerned. This last weakness is largely a heritage of their colonial past, which encouraged monocultures. These fundamental weaknesses should not lead the developing countries, however, to abstain from further efforts in this direction. In many cases and with regard to many problem areas, regional organizations of developing countries will be able to increase substantially the individual and collective degree of self-re-

liance and of economic and technical development of the countries concerned. The World Bank Group, regional development banks and other international economic organizations should therefore continue to assist the developing countries in the establishment of regional organizations. Free trade may then sometimes be a less important goal of such organizations than cooperation for development.

REFERENCES [*])

Roepke, W., "Economic order and international law", Red. d. C. Ac. Dr. Int. 1954, p. 207

Erler, G., Grundprobleme des internationalen Wirtschaftsrecht, Göttingen 1956.

l'Huillier, J.A., Théorie et pratique de la coopération économique internationale, Paris 1957.

Röling, B.V.A., International law in an expanded world, Amsterdam 1960.

Schwarzenberger, G., Economic world order? A basic problem of international economic law, Manchester 1970.

Meerhaeghe, M.A.G.van, International economic institutions, second edition, London 1972.

Nême, J. et C., Organisations économiques internationales, Paris 1972.

Bergsten, C.F. (ed.), The future of the international economic order, an agenda for research, Lexington (Mass.)-Toronto-London 1973.

Ladreit de la Charrière, G., "L'influence de l'inégalité de développement des Etats sur le droit international", Red. d. C. Ac. Dr. Int. 1973, p. 233

Tinbergen, J. (coord.), Reshaping the international order, New York 1976.

Kapteyn, P.J.G. and E.P.Wellenstein, De nieuwe internationale economische orde, Mededelingen van de Nederlandse Vereniging voor Internationaal Recht, no.75, September 1977.

---

[*]) In chronological order. Only books have been listed in this selected bibliography. Since the UN resolutions on a new international economic order of 1974, a flood of articles on the subject has appeared in all international law journals and many other legal, economic, foreign-policy and more interdisciplinary international journals like Round Table and International Organization. Because of the high quality of most of these articles, any selection would be arbitrary. An analysis of a great number of them will be given in my book, quoted at the end of the bibliography.

Schachter, O., <u>Sharing the World's Resources</u>, New York 1977.

Jacobson, H.K., <u>Networks of Interdependence: International Organizations and the Global Political System</u>, Alfred Knopf 1977.

VerLoren van Themaat, P., <u>Rechtsgrondslagen van een nieuwe internationale economische orde</u>, The Hague 1977.

2 ECONOMIC SELF-DETERMINATION AND HUMAN RIGHTS: SOME REMARKS

Gert-Jan Veerman and Paulien van der Ploeg-van Oort

2.1. INTRODUCTION

The first article of both Covenants on Human Rights (1966)
concerns the right of all peoples to self-determination. By
virtue of that right all peoples freely determine their political status and freely pursue their economic, social and cultural development. In the second section of article 1, economic self-determination, it is said: 'All peoples may, for their
own ends, freely dispose of their natural wealth and resources
without prejudice to any obligations arising out of international economic co-operation, based upon the principle of mutual benefit, and international law. In no case may a people
be deprived of its own means of subsistence'.
    Prima facie the relation between the first and the second
section of article 1, between political and economic self-
determination, is clear. In the first section the rights of
peoples to political independence have been recognized. However, more is needed. Along with political independence, economic independence is proclaimed as a right to which all peoples are entitles.
    Historically seen, this explanation is correct. Article 1
was drafted in the area of decolonization, in the 1950's.
Several peoples were then struggling for independence. Other
peoples had just won their politically independent status.
There was a growing consciousness that political independence
was not enough for determining their own development. A people
should also be independent economically, able to freely dispose of their natural wealth and resources. Without this economic self-reliance, political independence was considered to
be empty.
    In this interpretation the first two sections of article 1
are closely related. Two main aspects of decolonization were
fixed for the future, laid down as a right. In this light the
third section of article 1 makes sense. All States, especially
those having responsibility for the so-called "Non-Self-Govern-

ing Territories", are urged to further the realization of the right of those territories to self-determination. This section refers to the colonial situation expressly. This situation must come to an end by granting peoples the right to self-determination, politically and economically.

In this contribution this concept will be questioned. It is dubious for several reasons. The right to self-determination became part of the Covenants on Human Rights, documents which where and are intended to have a more durable significance (while political independence has already been won by all colonial territories).

Besides, it is very likely that the connection between self-determination and human rights, urged and wanted by the proclamation of self-determination in the UN Covenants on Human Rights, will stimulate a new meaning of and scope for, or a new emphasis on, the concept of self-determination, politically and economically. Also, the view that self-determination merely implies the independence of colonial territories is open to doubt. Historically, for instance, it is possible to consider other manifestations of the idea of self-determination. In this connection the question can be raised whether self-determination can be applied to colonies, whereas it is considered to refer to nations and peoples.

These are reasons enough for a somewhat deeper investigation into the concept of self-determination, as laid down in the Covenants on Human Rights.

In Section 2.2. we will have a look at the development of the concept of economic self-determination. This development will be described mainly by referring to resolutions of the UN General Assembly.

The third section deals with the idea of political self-determination. Here, attention will also be paid to the notion of the nation and to the concept of human rights.

In Section 2.4. we will try to set out some lines for the possible significance of economic self-determination, in the light of its relation to political self-determination and human rights. This is summarized in Section 2.5. ('Concluding Remarks').

2.2. ECONOMIC SELF-DETERMINATION

Article 1 of both Covenants on Human Rights was drafted in the early 1950's, when decolonization was a major topic. In 1951 the General Assembly decided that an article concerning the right to self-determination should be inserted in the draft Covenant(s) on Human Rights. The text of the article, as drafted by the Human Rights Commission, contained the political aspect of the right to self-determination and the present third section of article 1. The right of peoples to self-determination, it was further stated, should include permanent sovereignty over their natural wealth and resources. (1) It was intended that self-determination should be envisaged from an economic point of view too, since political independence was based on economic independence. Therefore, the right

of peoples to their natural wealth and resources should be
recognized. An article concerning self-determination in relation to civil and political rights would be worthless unless
it was also applied to economic rights.

In 1955 the Third Committee of the General Assembly had
time to discuss the draft text of article 1. (2) The inclusion of economic self-determination was not everybody's wish.
One of the objections was that the term 'permanent sovereignty' had little meaning. Besides, the warning was given that
the provision might discourage foreign investors and could
harm the policy of assistance to underdeveloped countries.

A special working group for redrafting the text proposed
the final text of article 1 after six meetings. (3) It was
adopted by 33 States to 12, with 13 abstentions. The Western
world voted against it.

The General Assembly, after postponing it in 1955, 1956 and
1957, referred the question of self-determination to the Third
Committee, where in 1958 another discussion took place. Again,
consensus could not be found. It was argued that the principle
of self-determination had nothing to do with control over natural resources, which was an essential attribute of sovereignty. It was harmful for the encouragement of the international
flow of private capital. Another argument 'found' was that it
was illogical to use the word 'sovereignty' in reference to
peoples which did not yet make up sovereign States. (4)

Other representatives stated that the permanent sovereignty
of natural wealth and resources was of the utmost importance
to underdeveloped countries. Insertion of an article like this
was necessary, they said, because it was an essential element
of the right of self-determination, namely that no people subjected to foreign economic domination could be deemed independent.

Economic self-determination, i.e. permanent sovereignty
over natural wealth and resources, was considered to be very
important, although its precise meaning was not very clear.
The discussion on economic self-determination stopped too soon,
however, at least in its relation to article 1 of the Covenants.
The text was finished. (5) The proposal was adopted by a roll-
call vote of 52 to 15 with 4 abstentions. The Western world
voted against.

The recommendations of the Third Committee to form a commission for further study on the subject was followed by the
General Assembly at the plenary meeting of 12 December, 1958.
By resolution 1314 (XIII) the Commission on Permanent Sovereignty over Natural Resources was installed.

In this resolution, with recommendations 'concerning international respect for the right of peoples and nations to self-
determination' the relation between self-determination and
permanent sovereignty is still present: 'Noting that the right
of peoples to self-determination as affirmed in the two draft
Covenants completed by the Commission on Human Rights includes
permanent sovereignty over their natural wealth and resources...'. This is also true for the result of the activities of
the Commission on Permanent Sovereignty, namely GA resolution
1803 (XVII), containing 8 articles on permanent sovereignty

over natural resources. (6) In the preamble permanent sovereignty over natural resources is called 'a basic constituent
of the right to self-determination'. In later resolutions
reference is made to these resolutions 1314 and 1803. But only
in these references can the connection be seen. The close relationship of economic self-determination and permanent sovereignty has actually been lost. Permanent sovereignty as such
is an issue again. (7) This issue was further developed in
the organs of the United Nations.

The first thing which is rather significant is the emphasis
on the sovereignty of States. The importance of sovereignty
had appeared already earlier. In GA resolution 626 (VII) it
was stated: 'Remembering that the right of peoples freely to
use and exploit their natural wealth and resources is inherent in their sovereignty'. Sovereignty was the starting point
for economic development. This also becomes clear when one
considers the statement of some countries, mostly from the
Third World, that it was not necessary to lay down the related
right to nationalization of natural resources. This was already an attribute of sovereignty, and by laying down this
kind of sovereignty one would weaken the right of all sovereign States to permanent sovereignty over their natural resources implicitly. Sovereign rights need not be codified.
The representative of Mexico used these words: They were 'unable to accept the last paragraph [of resolution 626], which
recommended that Member States should "recognize" the right
of each country to nationalize and freely exploit its natural
wealth. It was not for the United Nations to pass judgment on
a principle of unquestionable validity. Countries which were
so authorized by their constitutions could exercise the right
of nationalization on the same grounds as they exercised the
right to levy taxes or to summon their nationals to arms, and
there was no need for any international organization to recognize that right!
    Also in resolution 1803 (XVII) sovereignty is the central
focus. But the States disagreed about the reach of this sovereignty. The discussion circled round two essential principles: respect for the national sovereignty of developing countries in need of foreign capital for the development of their
natural resources, and the provision of adequate guarantees
for potential investors. (8) The latter view was held by the
Western States. They succeeded in adding the remark that sovereignty finds its limits in rules of international law. After
resolution 1803, it has been made clear many times that the
sovereignty over natural wealth and resources belongs to the
overall sovereignty of the States (see, for example, resolutions 2158 (XXI), 2386 (XXIII), 2692 (XXV), 3016 (XXVII),
3171 (XXVIII)). This is also true for the resolutions in which
the progressive development of international economic relations is stipulated, in order to solve the problems of, for
example, poverty and underdevelopment, the resolutions concerning the New International Economic Order (3201 (S-VI) and
3202 (S-VI) and the Charter of Economic Rights and Duties of
States (3281 (XXIX)). The relations between States is the is-

sue in those resolutions; the starting point is equal sovereignty. From this position of formal equality the development to a more factual equality is urged. The meaning of sovereignty has even been extended: in comparison with resolution
1803 (XVII), which was long seen as indicative, there is a difference. The reference to international law, one of the favour-
ite subjects of the Western world, has disappeared. The emphasis on sovereignty seemed to be even stronger. (9)

These remarks concerned the importance of sovereignty in
the international economic order as a sequel to economic self-
determination. Also the object of permanent sovereignty is
developed.

In the first place more natural wealth and resources were
included - according to the technical possibilities - such as
the wealth of the sea. See, for instance, GA resolutions 3016
(XXVII) and 3171 (XXVIII): the General Assembly affirms 'the
rights of States to permanent sovereignty over all their natural resources, on land within their international boundaries,
as well as those found in the seabed and the subsoil thereof
within their national jurisdiction and in the superjacent wa-
ters'. (10)

Another example of the extension of the object of permanent
sovereignty is the control over a complete economic process;
permanent sovereignty covers all stages, from exploration to
marketing (see e.g. resolution 3171 (XXVIII). In the Declaration on the New International Economic Order (under e), the
permanent sovereignty over natural resources and all economic
activities is recorded. Article 2 gives an elaboration. (11)
The Declaration on Economic Rights and Duties of States contains a similar statement.

The conclusion of this section may be that economic self-
determination was inserted in the Covenants on Human Rights,
where it, more specifically, was defined as the permanent sovereignty over natural wealth and resources. Permanent sovereignty became an important issue in the regulation of international economic relations. Also in the new ways which were
developed to solve international economic problems, permanent
sovereignty is a basis. Its relation with political self-determination and human rights, however, was not, as it seems, elab-
orated.

2.3. POLITICAL SELF-DETERMINATION AND HUMAN RIGHTS (12)

2.3.1. Introduction

The explanation of article 1 of the Covenants on Human Rights
given in the Introduction of this contribution, was that self-
determination means the right of peoples of colonial territories to independent statehood. We considered this concept to be
open to doubt. One question is whether the definition of the
subject is correct. In practice people living within colonial
areas won independence; in the literature, however, such a definition is, as far as we know, unknown.

Secondly, one may ask whether it is correct to consider

self-determination as the act of gaining independent statehood. Historically, other ideas about and manifestations of
the principle of self-determination have existed. This raises
another question, namely, whether this concept of self-determination has not a too limited scope and future, because self-
determination would loose its meaning after decolonization. In
this respect one may also refer to the fact that self-determination was taken into the context of human rights by the
United Nations.

In this section we will pay attention to the subject of
self-determination (2.3.2.), to the development of the concept of self-determination (2.3.3.) and to the concept of human rights (2.3.4.).

2.3.2. The subject of self-determination

The subject of self-determination is called 'people' of 'nation'. (13) In this contribution we will not go deeply into
the notion of the nation and the problems of its operational-
ization. For a better understanding of this section it is,
however, necessary to make at least a few remarks.

In Western common language 'nation' can be synonymous with
'State'. Although there are some arguments for this identity,
we think these concepts have to be separated. The identifica-
tion is a simplification. 'State' refers to an organization,
'nation' to a people. Sometimes the State originated the nation; many times a 'nation' was the basis for a State. Etymo-
logically the two concepts differ too. 'Nation' was originally
understood as a community of descent; it implied a more or
less natural group of people. The word 'State' had more to do
with status, position; it has a statical connotation.

The close connection between State and nation is due to the
French Revolution. The juridical meaning of 'nation' implied
the leading groups in the State. During the French Revolution
the Third Estate wished to take over that leading position,
wanted to be that 'nation' as a counterpart to the king. It
wanted democracy. The State became the cause of the nation
(the Third Estate or the whole people -- in theory). This
democratic ideal moved to Central and Eastern Europe where the
frontiers of States and those of so-called cultural nations
differed widely. Politically, the dominated nations in those
parts of Europe asked for liberation and wished to give shape
to their cultural nationhood (which had earlier been evolved
under the influence of German Romanticism. Every - cultural -
nation should have an own State. In this view a nation was a
community of people who shared common features, such as language, religion, culture or history (later a subjective element
was sometimes added).

Also the meaning of the people belonging to a State (the
citizens of a State) was developed. In both circumscriptions
reference is made to people as individuals. (14)

In the United Nations the problem of defining the nation
existed too. No definition was found. As Third World spokesmen
said: a definition is not necessary, all peoples have the right

to self-determination. In practice, they were the inhabitants of colonial territories; the administrative area ruled in fact.

In this article we will consider 'nations' or 'peoples' as the inhabitants of the States, as a whole and in the group to which they belong.

2.3.3. The concept of self-determination

Self-determination is, in our view, an - old - principle of internal regulation of the State. It is the expression of the idea of the sovereign power of the people or, in more American terminology, the consent of those governed. This idea can be found at the time of the American and French Revolutions of the eighteenth century. At that time sovereignty was asked for by certain groups of society. In France the Third Estate wished to take over the leading position in the State, wanted to be that 'nation' as a counterpart to the King. It wanted democracy. The citizens should have the power with regard to the polity. These political wishes were opposed to the state of affairs known as the 'Ancien Régime'. This regime, a declining absolute monarchy, was felt as an impediment to the development of the citizens, politically and economically.

The new political attitude was based on the then prevailing natural law theories, in conformance to which sovereignty was deducted from the consent of those governed. Sovereignty was considered to be vested in the people. Now the question is, how self-determination did get connected with the idea of independent statehood. This was due to a development of that democratic principle in the nineteenth century. The ideal of the sovereign power of the people was spread over Europe. In Middle and Eastern Europe the 'nation' as a cultural concept was gaining importance, influenced by German Romanticism and often in reaction to suppression. A 'people' was the naturally-developed entity to which individuals belonged. Especially language was a decisive factor; language was the expression of the spirit of the people. To the advocates of the cultural nation, popular sovereignty meant an own government for the own people (in a cultural sense). (15)

Every - cultural - nation should decide on its own future. In other words, the political ideal of Enlightenment had been taken over; the subject of sovereignty was changed. The culturally-defined nation was considered to be the most logical unit for sovereignty.

This mingling of democracy and nationalism led to a specific concept of self-determination. This was actualized in the independence of several European and Latin-American territories. Sometimes it implied secession from the existing State (e.g. groups in the Ottoman or Austrian Empires); sometimes groups sought for unification (as in the cases of Germany and Italy). As we said, this specific concept of national self-determination was derived from the more general idea of self-determination, i.e. the consent of those governed. Paradoxically, the specific concept was at the same time contrary to that general idea. Sovereignty was vested in the nation, the governors were

governing by consent of the people. Thus, the general idea.
Regarding the principle of nationalism, however, sovereignty
was legitimized by the nation, a category which was highly independent of the will of the people. The nation was mainly determined by factors such as language, religion or culture.
   It should also be noted that the national idea of 'every
nation its own State' was never realized. Even the national
States which were the result of a nationalist movement contained groups within their frontiers which were easy to define
as peoples in a cultural sense.

With 'independence' the meaning and scope of self-determination is not exhausted, from a historical point of view. In the
nineteenth century other manifestations of the ideals of democracy and nationalism existed. Plebiscites were held, areas won
territorial autonomy, some minorities were protected as
such. (16) The latter meant the granting of special rights
(such as freedom of worship, education, the use of language)
to groups which differed from the majority of the population.
In the nineteenth century this concept of the protection of
minorities was applied at the Congress of Berlin of 1878,
where several Ottoman territories became independent States
(e.g. Romania).
   For this century self-determination played an important role
in the World War I. During the war the struggling parties devoted themselves to the realization of self-determination.
Woodrow Wilson declared that the right of people to self-determination should be the basis of the peace settlement after
the war. In his Fourteen Points he mentioned the restoration
of the sovereignty of Belgium (pt. 7), the autonomous development of the peoples of the Habsburg Empire (pt. 10) and of the
non-Turkish peoples within the Ottoman Empire (pt. 12). Conforming to the American tradition, he considered self-determination primarily as meaning the consent of those governed:
'The settlement of every question of territory, of sovereignty, of economic arrangement [!], or of political relationship
upon the basis of the acceptance of that people immediately
concerned'. (17) Self-determination did not extend to colonial
peoples, in Wilson's opinion. That is to say, it did not imply their independence. (18)
   The peace settlement itself provided for, among other
things, the independence of Czechoslovakia, foreseen in some
plebiscites and in the arrangement of protection or minorities
in the Balkan States. In the Charter of the League of Nations,
however, no reference was made to self-determination.
   After World War II self-determination won a definite place
as a concept in international law in the UN Charter (article 1
(2)). This does not mean that a clear concept of self-determination existed. On the basis of the drafting history, article
1 (2) of the Charter can be interpreted as avowing democracy.
The purpose of the UN Charter, in connection with the Atlantic
Charter, was the restoration of democratic procedures. Article
1 (2) meant the real consent of those governed, based on a
free and genuine expression of their will. It was a statement
directed against fascist regimes. (19)

In the next period the right of peoples to self-determination was proclaimed many times, in service of decolonization.
All colonial territories should attain independent statehood.
This culminated in the famous Declaration on the Granting of
Independence to Colonial Peoples and Countries (GA resolution
1514). Following this declaration all colonial peoples have
the right to independence (or even the duty to become independent). And now most colonial territories have become independent States indeed. In the last twenty years we find, at the
same time, emphasis on independence, sovereignty, national
unity and territorial integrity. After decolonization, self-
determination seemed to have lost its significance for the
State concerned. Once independent, self-determination seemed
to be meaningless for the people involved. Self-determination
meant - again - only the act of winning independent statehood.
But, as we saw, the idea of self-determination is broader,
seen in its historical context. Also for the future, that
other part of history, this meaning of self-determination is
not the only one. To confirm this, one may point to some recent trends in international law and to the connection with
the concept of human rights (section 2.3.4.) by the inclusion
of self-determination in the Covenants on Human Rights.

Before elaborating this, it is good to say that decolonization as such is a realization of the principle of self-determination considered as an expression of the sovereign power
of those governed. It is the restoration of long lost sovereignty. Decolonization also reflects the function of self-determination: the resistance to alien domination and subjugation.

The first tendency we want to mention is the inclusion of
the right to self-determination in international documents
which are meant to outlive decolonization. We think of the Covenants on Human Rights and of the Declaration on Principles of
International Law Concerning Friendly Relations and Coopera-
tions among States. Secondly, not only the inadmissibility of
actions against territorial integrity (20), but also the qua-
lification of the minority regimes in South Africa and South
Rhodesia (Zimbabwe) as contrary to self-determination and
human rights, and the alleged ideal of countries in the Third
World to create free, multi-radical societies, refer to a continuous process of participation in polity and policy. Thirdly,
one may refer to the general formulation of self-determination. The definition of self-determination given by the UN
General Assembly is not restricted to colonies. It also holds
true for the functional circumscription: alien domination and
subjugation is contrary to self-determination and the rights
of man. 'Alien' must be understood as 'not in conformity with
the wishes of the people' (see also the GA resolutions on South
Africa and South Rhodesia). Not only was the colonial situation a form of alien domination, but dictatorship, too, can be
regarded as such.

This argumentation is supported by a renewed formulation of
self-determination in GA resolution 2625. In the last paragraph of the principle of equal rights and self-determination
of peoples, it is stated that it is forbidden to encourage or
legalize any action which threatens the territorial integrity

and political unity of sovereign States 'conducting themselves in compliance with the principles of equal rights and self-
determination of peoples as described above and <u>thus possessed
of a government representing the whole people belonging to the
territory without discrimination as to race, creed or colour</u>'.
In other words, self-determination also has relevance for
international relations within the State. It has to do with
situations of structural violence; it supports people in their
struggle against dictatorship, racial discrimination and various forms of alien domination.

For this meaning of self-determination, which outlives decolonization, more evidence is available. In the first place
it is, of course, closely linked with the - old - general idea
of self-determination (see above, section 2.3.3.). In the second place this meaning of self-determination fits the concept
of human rights. That concept is the subject of the next section.

2.3.4. Self-determination and human rights

In 1966 self-determination was proclaimed in both Covenants on
Human Rights. Therefore, we will pay some attention to the concept of human rights.

Human rights may, more substantially, be circumscribed as
those rights which form the juridical expression of the wishes
or needs of human beings to unfold the rights people consider
necessary to give full scope to themselves. Generally, human
rights are thought to be rights which give freedom from the
State in favour of the individual. It is possible, however, to
give a more specific meaning to the rights of man.

First of all, this specificity is the result of a functional
analysis of the history of the rights of man. Their function
appears to be 'regulation (adjustment) of power'. This implies
that it is dependent on the social context which human rights
are formulated and in what way. During the Middle Ages documents had already been drafted in Europe in which the power of
the king (lords, et cetera) was limited (e.g. Magna Carta
(1215), 'Joyeuse Entrée' (1356)). These agreements were intended to (re)affirm liberties and freedoms, necessary against the
tendency of growing centralization by the king. These liberties did not belong to individuals but to human beings, as
members of a group (e.g. a town). In the relatively static order, which was regarded as unchangeable, every person had a
position in conformity with the position of his group in society. This feature was absent in the individual and universal
rights, based on natural law, of the eighteenth and nineteenth
centuries. If we trace the development from collective rights
to individual rights we find a growing self-consciousness and
individualization, starting with businessmen who grew rich in
commerce. Money became more important for one's position; education became broader; people discovered that a social order
was not unchangeable. This also resulted in a growing demand
for responsibility and power. In this connection one may think

of the Renaissance, Humanism, the Reformation and the Enlightenment.

The United States' Declaration of Independence, which contains mention of some human rights, was directed against the tax legislation of remote England, which treated her American colonies as colonies indeed. The secession was a resistance against foreign (alien) domination. To explain individual rights in the first documents, one may refer to the influence of John Locke and to the situation of the Pilgrim Fathers, which had some resemblance to Locke's theoretical construction (in an unsettled area they founded communities, political entities to protect their lives and property).

In France the situation was different. The French Revolution was a reaction, mainly of the Third Estate, to absolute monarchy and feudal society. The citizens lived in an - economically - restricting social order in which they had to pay for the expenses of the king without having much political power. In contrast to the particular liberties and freedoms of particular groups, freedom had to become a general, abstract freedom from.... Social divisions had to disappear and the combination of private and political affairs had to be dissolved.

If those two revolutions were reactions to restricting social orders, reaction was also a feature of the next stage in the development of human rights in the nineteenth century. This time the issue was the regulation of social-economic powers (for instance the result of a development of industrialization and accumulation of capital in a liberal society in which freedom from the State) desired by groups who were powerless and economically bound. The so-called conflict between liberal ideas and social reality led to claims to social human rights, to measures necessary to make abstract and formal freedom a concrete and actual one.

Nowadays one may discover a tendency to claims to 'real democracy' instead of the existing formal democracy. There is a tendency to more participation in trade and industry in the extension of democratic procedures. This tendency may be regarded as a reaction to the growing feeling of powerlessness among people whose potentialities have increased. In general it is possible to maintain that groups of people (mostly a kind of sub-élite) claim rights when a discrepancy exists between their potentialities and social opportunities, when the discrepancy between ideal and reality is felt to be oppressive.

The function of human rights, that is to say the regulation of power, can also be found in the documents of the American and French Revolutions. We will mention three aspects.

In the first place, these documents state explicitly the reaction to the previous situations, that is to the English domination and the feudal structure of the 'Ancien Régime'.

In the second place, there is a structural aspect:
- the principle of sovereign power of the people: sovereignty belongs to the 'nation' and is not reserved for special sections of society;
- the idea that laws are equally binding for everybody: people

are not subject to the particular rules of particular persons;
- the separation of powers, which is the coping stone: concentration of power in one hand will be impossible.

In the third place, this structural aspect has a complement: it is meant to secure human rights. Human rights (freedom) were the reason for instituting this kind of political society.

After this historical analysis of human rights we come to the second reason for a more specific meaning of the rights of man.

Freedom, the aim of the liberal political structure, was conceived to be a general freedom from... (which is said to be the meaning and scope of the rights of man). It is known that the liberal conception of freedom has been criticized. The first criticism can be found in the social results of the liberal idea of freedom. As mentioned before, freedom in social life led to a lack of freedom and power for most people, to poverty and alienation.

An anthropological criticism was given by Karl Marx. Among other things he sharply attacked the division of human beings into 'hommes' and 'citizens' as well as the idea that human beings are each other's limitation of freedom (the idea of people living apart together).

Raymond Aron points to other aspects of freedom, such as the right to participate in the political order and the power of individuals and collectivities to fulfil their wishes and achieve their ends.

Following this track one might say that freedom is related to 'power in one's own situation'. Power can be defined as 'potentiality', or, more specifically, as 'the possibility to have influence'. This proposition is supported by our historical examination of human rights: the struggle of certain groups for more power was a struggle for more rights (or vice versa).

Another way of laying down the relation between freedom and power is through the concept of 'responsibility'. Parallel to the development of individualization and growing self-consciousness was a tendency to a more individual responsibility for one's own life. The religious or ethical demand for human beings to be responsible with regard to their environment, their lives and the lives of others, implies power. In order to be responsible and to be made responsible, one must have had influence on the decisions taken.

One can also mention the modern anthropological way of thinking: human beings are partly conditioned by their culture, et cetera, and partly open to the future. Man, together with his fellow men, shapes himself and his culture. For this he possesses the potentiality (power!) and needs responsibility.

Human rights are thus related to the chain freedom - power - responsibility. The regulation of the powers appeared to be the function of human rights; people reacted to domination by others, asked for human rights so as to create a situation which makes their unfolding possible and gives structure to their conditions. In this sense every person possesses a certain sovereignty, a certain power in his human rights.

Summarizing this section, we will mention, firstly, that the relation between self-determination and human rights is a rather old one. Self-determination as an expression of the idea that the sovereign power of the people was closely linked with individual freedoms. Personal freedom and autonomy, the alleged aim of the rights of man, implied the power to give consent to the laws of society. In its general sense self-determination is the right of citizens to participate in polity and policy. In the nineteenth century this democratic idea, the legitimation of the rulers, was connected with the national idea. This led to a more specific meaning of self-determination. The second outcome is that, considering the function of human rights, individuals have a right to control their situation, especially when they consider themselves dominated. In the third place one may also conclude that both self-determination and human rights imply a certain autonomy of groups to which people belong and the possibility of influencing the policy of the government and the form of government.

So self-determination as a general idea and as a specific concept is to be realized within the State.

2.4. A NEW SCOPE FOR ECONOMIC SELF-DETERMINATION?

In this contribution it should become clear that economic self-determination as such means the permanent sovereignty of nations over their natural wealth and resources. This concept was developed extensively; the object of permanent sovereignty widened more and more, verbally resulting in a sovereignty over all economic activities. What remained was the focus on national sovereignty. If one makes a distinction between an internal and an external aspect of sovereignty, economic self-determination would appear to be a part of the external side. It was of importance in international relations. The New International Economic Order is also based upon the sovereignty of the participating States.

In this point of view economic self-determination has only little relevance for the question of human rights, even though it was proclaimed in both Covenants on Human Rights. The insertion of economic self-determination in both Covenants came about because political self-determination (seen as the right to independence for colonial territories) was considered to be empty without an economic complement.

This could be the conclusion of this study on economic self-determination as defined in the first article of the Covenants on Human Rights. With such a conclusion we are, however, not very content; there is more to be said. Could economic self-determination have an internal aspect too? Could it have relevance for internal economic relations within the State? And if so, what does this mean?

For an affirmative answer on the first question one may point to the insertion of economic self-determination in the

UN Covenants in the first place. Human rights are to be implemented in the national field. They work primarily in the relations between citizens and government.

A second reason for further investigation in the relevance
of economic self-determination for internal economic relations
is due to the concept of self-determination and to the development of the right of self-determination lately. As pointed out,
political self-determination is mainly a principle of internal
regulation of the State. It means the right to participation
in policy and polity. In this sense the subject of self-determination is the people within the State, and not the State itself. A growing discrepancy between political and economic
self-determination is the result of both developments. This
discrepancy would diminish if economic self-determination were
also related to the people within the State. Besides, since
economic self-determination was seen as the component of political self-determination, one may assume that the development
of political self-determination should influence the meaning
of that other aspect of the general idea of self-determination.

In this connection we also want to point to the wording of
article 1 of the Covenants, in which self-determination also
means the right 'freely to pursue [the] own economic, social
and cultural development'. (21)

The UN General Assembly resolutions concerning permanent
sovereignty do not exclude the relevance of economic self-
determination in internal economic relations. The fourth principle on which the new International Economic Order should be
founded (d) is 'the right of every country to adopt the economic and social system that it deems the most appropriate for
its own development and not to be subjected to discrimination
of any kind as a result. Neither is the indicated subject of
economic self-determination an impediment for the view that it
also has an internal side. As we saw (in Section 2.3.2.) the
word 'nation' preferably has the meaning of the people inhabit-
ing the State. 'Nation' refers in principle to the personal
substrate of the State. This can also be true for the subject
of economic self-determination. Not the territories but the
peoples of those territories were to become independent, politically and economically.

In the Declaration on the New International Economic Order,
reference is made to the people within the State. In operative
paragraph 1 it is said that the remaining vestiges of alien
and colonial domination, foreign occupation, racial discrimination, apartheid and neo-colonialism in all its forms continue
to be among the greatest obstacles to the full emancipation
and progress of the developing countries and all the peoples
involved. Also the principles h) and i) speak of the right of
the developing countries and the peoples of territories under
colonial and alien (or racial) domination (et cetera). (22)

We cannot see why the subject of self-determination should
change, immediately after the (re)gaining of effective control
and sovereignty by the people, into the State. This the more
since the concept of 'nation' does not urge such a change and
an analysis of the history of self-determination shows that
self-determination regards the people or the peoples within

the State. Also, in another respect, the New International
Economic Order does not impede concern for the international
side of economic self-determination. The goal of this Order
is not to strengthen the sovereignty of States, but to further the national development and the well-being of the
people concerned. The goal is 'the full emancipation and progress of the developing countries and all the peoples involved'. Recently it was stated (in GA resolution 32/130, para.
1) that 'the realization of the New International Economic
Order is an essential element for the effective promotion of
human rights and fundamental freedoms...'. Besides one may consider that this goal of the New International Economic Order
will cause changes in the political and economic structure
within the States. An Order which only guarantees freedom
from want to an élite, and does not contribute to the development of all people, is not the Order meant.

Now that we have tried to legitimize economic self-determination as applicable to internal economic relations, the question is what that appropriateness involves. We are not able to
give a sharp and precise answer, but shall try to outline some
aspects.

Both the concepts of self-determination and human rights
express, functionally seen, resistance to foreign domination.
More substantially, both are necessary to give full scope to
people. Both imply power over one's own present and future
situation. This power extends to polity (the general idea of
self-determination/popular sovereignty), to the several groups
in which human beings live necessarily (the specific meaning
of self-determination) and to the individuals as individuals.
This opinion for the right to participation in policy and
polity is not only of a political character. It extends to the
economic field too. First of all, of course, in the external
sense that others, such as multinationals or foreign States,
are excluded. But also in that it is up to the people to decide on economic development. To be more concrete, one may
think of parliamentary control or the like over decisions in
the economic field on the macro level. But for the lower
levels too one can imagine structures in which the peoples
concerned - which may be peoples in an ethnic sense, but also
peoples working in an area or in factories - have a say in the
way they (will) live their lives and produce their goods.

The function of self-determination appeared to be resistance
(now the legitimate resistance) to overwhelming structures, to
alien domination. This also holds true for economic self-determination. With this one can oppose the economic élites. Economic self-determination is, as said, also related to the concept of human rights. Human rights are necessary for the development of individuals in all aspects. Therefore many kinds
of human rights are recognized. Human rights imply the power
and the responsibility of individuals and groups for their
situation. This brings about minimum conditions for the internal and external economic order. In this respect we will refer
to an essential element of human rights: the equality of all
human beings. If economy is to be defined as the production
and distribution of welfare, this feature of human rights im-

plies the fair distribution of this welfare. (23) For such a
fair distribution another reason also exists. Economic discrimination is one of the reasons peoples manifest themselves
and ask (and fight) for their national self-determination. The
struggle for 'national liberation' is, certainly, fought under
the banner of national identity, of nationhood. But among the
factors which cause such struggles the economic factor is an
important one. One may point to the conflicts arising around
the Kurds, to renewed Scottish efforts at nationalism or to
the expressed wishes for independence in Bougainville.

A fair share in the national income and attention for the
development of the - regional - economy is of major importance
in the prevention of such conflicts. Oppression raises demands
for self-determination; people ask for their right to the
self-determination which they already possess.

So, on the grounds of economic self-determination, participation in economic development and sharing in its revenues are
necessary; they belong to the meaning of self-determination in
its internal aspect. Not only the relation to human rights
brings about that fair distribution of goods. Article 1 of
both Covenants provides expressis verbis for a minimum: 'In no
case may a people be deprived of its own means of subsistence'.
Why should this minimum only count in international relations?
(24)

About the best structures, economically seen, many views
exist. It is not the place here (nor are we able) to consider
these. Self-determination, especially economic self-determination, could be the juridical basis for structures in which the
participation of the people in economy and economic development of the polity is guaranteed. Or, in the words of article
1.1 of the Covenants, in which the people are able 'freely to
pursue their economic... development'.

This view on the significance of - economic - self-determination has some relevance to the question or the priority of
social and economic development, with which an autocratic
structure is often legitimized. It is, in this context, con-
tended that economic development has full priority. First of
all, people must have enough to eat. Participation, freedom
of expression and the like are articles of luxury.

Without denying the partial rightness of this latter remark,
we want to state that self-determination (that right which is
'a prerequisite to the enjoyment of all other human rights')
implies that people, that the citizens, are entitled to co-
operate and to participate in the development of the country.
Economic self-determination means the right to pursue freely
the own economic development. This includes, almost logically,
the direct concern of the people concerned.

In the vision given, political and economic self-determination are indeed still as closely related as they were, notwithstanding the rather autonomous development of the concept
of permanent sovereignty over natural resources. Externally,
the State is the sovereign actor; internally, however, sovereignty belongs to the people, conforming to the right of
self-determination.

2.5. CONCLUDING REMARKS

The second section of article 1 of the Covenants on Human Rights states that all peoples have sovereignty over their natural wealth and resources. This was first related to the populations of colonial territories; it came to emcompass the sovereignty of States. However, it is not necessary to delimit the scope of economic self-determination in that way. Self-determination is still attributed to the people, not to governments. Also the intent of economic self-determination as inserted in the Covenants does not bring about the state of affairs that States should be the only subjects of self-determination. Besides, the first section of article 1 notes the right of all peoples freely to pursue their economic development. (25) Article 1.1 can be seen as the general rule of - economic - self-determination; section 2 as a specification, including a minimum condition.

Economic self-determination as such has, in this view, relevance for internal economic relations. This internal aspect deserves more emphasis in studies on economic relations, since economic self-determination forms part of the general idea of self-determination, which is the participation of people in policy and polity, and since it has become the first of the human rights.

Human rights work primarily within the State. They express a goal meant to strengthen the freedom, the power and the responsibility of people for their conditions of life.

So the right to economic self-determination must be implemented within the countries of the world, rich and poor. Economic self-determination means that people are entitled to co-operate and to participate in the economic development and in the political and economic structure chosen for this development.

The New International Economic Order aims at new economic relations to combat poverty. This implies not only new international relations, but also new relations and structures within the States. Therefore self-determination provides the juridical basis.

FOOTNOTES

1. United Nations Yearbook, 1952, p. 440. Doc. E/2256,
   par. 91.

2. United Nations Yearbook, 1955, p. 155 ff. Doc. A/2929,
   Annotations on the text of the draft International Covenants on Human Rights, 1. July, 1955.

3. 'The peoples may, for their own ends, freely dispose of
   their natural wealth and resources without prejudice to
   any obligations arising out of international economic cooperation, based upon the principle of mutual benefit and
   international law. In no case may a people be deprived of
   its own means of subsistence.'

4. United Nations Yearbook, 1958, p. 213.

5. All peoples may for their own ends freely dispose of
   their natural wealth and resources without prejudice to
   any obligations arising out of international co-operation
   based upon the principle of mutual benefit and international law. In no case may a people be deprived of its
   own means of subsistence. The opposition of the Western
   countries concerned especially the related right of nationalization. The meaning of the reference to principles
   of international law was that they wanted to be sure compensation would follow a nationalization.

6. United Nations Yearbook, 1962, p. 499.

7. The issue of permanent sovereignty was dealt with in the
   2nd Cie of the G.A., for instance, and not in the 3rd Cie.

8. United Nations Yearbook, 1962, p. 500.

9. See G. Feuer, RGDIP, 1975, p. 290 ff.

10. See for this problem M. Flory, Droit International du Dé-
    veloppement, p. 282 ff.

11. See for the disconsensus and the attitude of the Western
    countries, de Waart, 'Permanent Sovereignty over Natural
    Resources as a Cornerstone for International Economic
    Rights and Duties', in: Netherlands International Law
    Review', Vol. XXIV, 1977, p. 311 ff.

12. This section is based on G.J. Veerman, Het Zelfbeschik-
    kingsrecht der Naties en de Rechten van de Mens (Self-
    determination and Human Rights - with a summary in Eng-
    lish), Amsterdam, 1977.

13. In this study we use these terms as synonyms.

14. For a survey concerning the theories which try to define the nation and for criticism of these theories, see Chapters II and III of Veerman's book. For the nation as subject of self-determination he has proposed the circumscription: 'a more or less homogeneous group of people who undertake political activities to change their conditions and to give shape to their future; often political action is the result of suppression felt'.

15. It should be noted that also among these peoples the educated and economically-developed citizens opposed the feudal structure. They found the legitimation of their movement at a cultural level.

16. See e.g. H.J. Roethof, Het Zelfbeschikkingsrecht der Nationaliteiten (The Right to Self-determination of Nationalities), Utrecht, 1951.

17. Mount Vernon Speech, 4 July, 1918.

18. See his Point Five.

19. Some other indications for this interpretation are the rejection of the Rolin amendment and the rejection of the right of secession whereby it was stated that self-determination is self-government.

20. Another trend, already mentioned, is the strengthening of territorial integrity. This means that other States do not have the right to intervene or to support secession movements. It does not exclude the possibility of internal self-determination.

21. The Commission on Human Rights concluded in 1952 that article 1.1 included permanent sovereignty, later set up as article 1.2. So, the general principle of - economic - self-determination keeps its value.

22. In e.g. G.A. resolutions 3336 (XXIX), 3516 (XXX) and 31/186 the permanent sovereignty over natural resources is attributed to the Arab peoples under Israelien occupation. Such a sovereignty is also recognized for Namibia (see G.A. resolution 3295 (XXIX), under IV-8). One could contend that the restoration of sovereignty lost is the case. However, this sovereignty is attributed to subjects which are at that moment not sovereign States.

23. Seen from the angle of development a similar conclusion can be drawn. The U.N. Committee on Development Planning wrote (1970) that the purpose of development, a better life for all sections of the population, implied the necessity in developing countries 'to eliminate inequalities in the distribution of wealth and income, and mass poverty and social injustice...

24. Also U.O. Umozurike, <u>Self-determination in International Law</u>, 1972, p. 211, mentions, in connection with the last sentence of article 1.2, the possibility of protection of people against their own - corrupt - government, even though he considers economic self-determination as concerning <u>inter</u>national relations.

25. We are aware that the political realization of this possible interpretation of (economic) self-determination is difficult.

REFERENCES

Armbruster, H., 'Selbstbestimmungsrecht', in: Strupp, K. and Schlochauer, H.J., <u>Wörterbuch des Völkerrechts</u>, III, Berlin, 1962-2.

Bowett, D.W., Self-determination and Political Rights in the Developing Countries, <u>Proc. ASIL</u>, 1966, p. 129 ff.

Brehme, G., <u>Souveränität der jungen Nationalstaaten über Naturreichtümer</u>, Berlin, 1967.

Dekker, I.F., 'The New International Economic Order and the Legal Relevance of Structural Violence', in: <u>Revue Belge de Droit International</u>, Vol. 12, nr. 2, 1976, <u>pp.</u> 466-498.

Emde Boas, M.J. van, 'Permanente Soevereiniteit over Natuurlijke Hulpbronnen', in: <u>Internationale Spectator</u>, 1963, p. 500 ff.

Flory, M., <u>Droit International du Développement</u>, Paris, 1977.

Roethof, H.J., '<u>Het Zelfbeschikkingsrecht der Nationaliteiten</u>', Utrecht, 1951.

Umozurike, U.O., <u>Self-determination in International Law</u>, 1972.

Veerman, G.J., <u>Het Zelfbeschikkingsrecht der Naties en de Rechten van de Mens</u>, Amsterdam, 1977.

Waart, P.J.I.M. de, 'Permanent Sovereignty over Natural Resources as a Cornerstone for International Economic Rights and Duties', in: <u>Netherlands International Law Review</u>, Vol. XXIV, 1977, Special Issue in Honour of A.J.P. Tammes.

Williams, D., 'Economic Development and Human Rights', in: <u>N.J.C.M. Bulletin</u>, Vol. 3, no. 11, September, 1978, p. 56 ff.

See also the two special numbers of <u>Civis Mundi</u>, 1977-6 and 1978-1, about 'Nationale Soevereiniteit en Zelfbeschikking', especially the contribution of B.V.A. Röling and J. Tinbergen.

3 SPECIFIC TENSIONS IN THE RELATIONSHIP BETWEEN MULTINATIONAL ENTERPRISES AND DEVELOPING COUNTRIES

Sylvain R. Plasschaert

3.1. INTRODUCTION

The relationship between the multinational enterprise (MNE) and the nation state is characterized by endemic tensions, escalating at times into open conflict. Generally speaking, the antagonism is much more intense in less-developed countries (LDC's) than in developed countries.

And yet, that antagonism may be somewhat paradoxical, at first glance, if one considers the following facts:

1. The role   of MNE's is much more important in developed countries than in LDC's, at least in absolute terms. Recent data about cumulative investments by American MNE's abroad indicate that only 21 percent or $ 29 billion,out of a grand total of $ 137 billion, is invested in the Third World. (1) However, data portraying the degree of penetration of foreign firms in the local economy (especially in the manufacturing sector) show a different state of affairs and may be more revealing. Thus, Reuber and associates found that in 1970 the rate of Foreign Direct Investment (FDI) to Gross National Product, stood at 1.05 for LDC's, as against 0.57 for developed economies. (2).

2. The controls which host countries operate with respect to MNE's are, on the whole, much more elaborate and strict in LDC's than in developed economies. Impediments are raised as regards the conditions of entry as well as those of subsequent operation. A hypothetical case could therefore conceivably have been made that, with such a variegated arsenal of control measures in operation, LDC's could henceforth indulge in a fairly relaxed attitude towards MNE's which they could consider to be under effective control. And yet,not only did controls in fact proliferate but a great number of nationalizations have oc-

46

curred, especially in the mineral field. The right to nationalize or expropriate foreign business property against
appropriate compensation and according to the laws of the
nationalizing country has been enshrined in the 1974
Charter of Rights and Obligations of States (art.2, 2)c).

3. The attitude of nation states towards FDI and MNE is frequently somewhat ambiguous and cast in an uneasy relationship. On the one hand, there is widespread suspicion about
the motives and criticism of the operations of MNE. Animosity tends to be particularly rampant with various social
groups and even stretches across the ideological spectrum,
e.g. in labour unions (where allowed to operate), among
intellectuals, local businessmen and politicians (especially when belonging to the opposition). The control measures just mentioned reflect that critical attitude. On
the other hand, most governments proclaim that they wel-
come FDI; to this effect they tend to grant generous tax
and financial incentives.

The present essay is a modest contribution towards clarifying
whether specific factors or circumstances can be identified
which explain the tense relationship between LDC's and MNE.
In other words, an effort is made to isolate specific causes
of tension between MNE and LDC, in the sense that such anta-
gonisms are related both to the multinationality of firms and
the state of underdevelopment of the host country. In other
words, tensions that exist on a wide scale between governments and domestic firms, on the one hand, and between MNE
and governments of high-income countries, on the other, do
not satisfy the twofold standard just mentioned.
    My interest in the subject matter of this paper derives
from consideration of the paradoxes just mentioned; and from
the observation that in the heated discussions about MNE, arguments are frequently advanced which are obviously not uni-
quely related to MNE or to LDC. As J.Dunning and M.Gilman
recently stated: "In many cases, it is unclear whether the
perceived conflicts result from the 'multinationality' of
these firms or from the fact that they are foreign, big, private, or Western, or efficient (thus challenging local mono-
polists) or oligopolistic". (3)
    The approach is predominantly deductive, based on an over-
view of a number of features of the LDC and the MNE that appear to be relevant. The two causes of tension that may be
deemed specific in the relationship between LCD and MNE are
subsequently discussed at some length. They refer to the
"ownership" (and related "control") issue and to the alleged
inappropriateness of the product mix of MNE to cater to the
priority needs of LDC. Frequent references will be made in text
and footnotes to theoretical and empirical work on LDC and
MNE. Although no comprehensive treatment of the issues covered could be attempted within the limited scope of this
paper, hopefully, some of the preliminary findings may suggest areas of further fruitful research. In this context,
one should mention that factual evidence on the role of MNE's
in LDC's is still fragmentary and often contradictory. (4)

One additional preliminary caveat is in order. Both the MNE and the LDC are viewed here in a generic sense, although both cover a wide spectrum. Economic sectors display widely varying features and the strategies of, for example, Nestlé or Unilever, are bound to significantly differ from those of IBM or Philips. As a casual look at the UN-data on per capita incomes suggests, the differentiation amongst LDC's has become more prominent in recent years. Countries with an "intermediate" income per capita level that tops, say, $ 500, typically appear in a position to develop a fairly diversified industry (5) and a growing middle class, i.e. one with a per capita income level well above subsistence needs. The degree of control of MNE's also substantially differs among the countries of the Third World. Generally speaking, however, we may confidently assume that although several IDC's have consistently welcomed FDI, the uneasy relationship already mentioned prevails on the whole.

3.2. BASIC FEATURES OF LESS-DEVELOPED COUNTRIES

LDC's as a group, i.e. abstracting upon significant differences of degree in the situation of individual countries, could, in our view, be characterized by the following basic features. As the latter are rather straightforward and have been amply covered in the literature, there is no need to dwell on them at length.

3.2.1. Poverty and a segmented economy

Generally speaking, the population of a developing country is poor and the economy is segmented into different, ill-connected subsystems. Poverty, obviously, has a comparative connotation. The average per capita income of poor countries in the "South" lies far below that of rich countries in the "North". But there also exists an absolute dimension to poverty. Large masses, and indeed the majority of the population in many LDC's do not or only barely reach a per capita income level above "absolute poverty". (6) Absolute poverty consists in an utterly inadequate amount of income and purchasing power but also in insufficient educational and health facilities and other essential "public services". Generally, no possibility exists for escaping from the harsh and hopeless "culture of poverty". (7) The combination of a low per capita income and of a frequently skewed distribution of income levels implies that only a small segment of the population has the purchasing power which affords an affluent, Northern consumption pattern.

The stark contrast between the comparatively few "haves" and the many "have-nots" is one major aspect of the segmented economy. The fragmentation also involves the dichotomy between
a. modern urban centres on the one hand, and the squalid fringes of the cities and the backward countryside on the other;

b. regions of widely different levels of development, if not
   of natural potential; and
c. small, fairly modern, high-productivity industrial and
   service sectors and more traditional low-productivity
   ways of production in both agriculture and in industry
   (as is the case with the cottage and handicraft sectors).

3.2.2. A rather "flat" profile of manufacturing industry

Modern mechanized industry tends to be concentrated largely
in the sector of fairly simple consumer goods; there is little capital "deepening", i.e. local production of capital
goods - except in larger LDC's such as Brazil or India. Local industrial ventures, resulting both from domestic and
foreign initiatives, tend to be heavily protected against
competing imports.

3.2.3. Technological lag and dependence

Invention and innovation of new products and more efficient
production processes typically occur in the high-income
North, where there are dense concentrations of R and D activities. Hence, LDC's are basically cast in the role of dependent recipients of technology which is developed elsewhere.

3.2.4. Emphasis upon economic growth

Amongst the economic objectives of governments in LDC's one
goal, viz. rapid economic growth, clearly stands out. It
frequently tends to be pursued at the peril of neglecting
other stated objectives such as price stability or a less
unequal distribution (to which only lip-service may be
paid).

3.2.5. A strong nationalist stance

Both in economic and political matters, governments tend to
defend strong nationalist positions. Nationalist feelings
are instilled as a catalyst in the frequently arduous process of nation-building and in expressing a country's unique
identity. In the economic sphere poor countries, acting increasingly as a more compact group, seek a more equitable
international distribution of income and wealth, in what has
been termed a "new international economic order".

3.2.6. Non-western cultures

Modern economic development, triggered by the agricultural
and industrial "revolutions", had its roots in 18th century

Western Europe and later in the United States. Most poor
countries today are located in the non-Western world and are
imbued with their own non-Western cultures and cultural heritage, cherishing the traditions and values they naturally
want to preserve against excessive intrusion of alien values
or life-styles. (8)

3.3. RELEVANT FEATURES OF MULTINATIONAL ENTERPRISES

The following features appear to reflect quite accurately
the general profile of MNE's and are also directly relevant
to our enquiry. I focus on MNE's which are large by such
standards as overall turnover or profits. (Quite a few MNE's
- as conventionally defined, i.e. enterprises with at least
one producing affiliate abroad - are of small dimensions).

3.3.1. Western enterprises

The headquarters of most MNE's are still located almost exclusively in the developed countries of the non-Socialist
world. American-based MNE's dominate, according to U.N. data.
Japanese and German outward FDI are also on the rise.

3.3.2. Frequently a superior position

MNE's frequently display a superior position in LDC's vis-à-
vis local competing firms. They may employ production techniques not yet accessible to the local firms, as in the case
of the capital goods sector, and an international brand name
may have a strong appeal not necessarily derived from its
intrinsic qualities. The MNE usually has the advantage of
having previously tested production and marketing of the
product in its own home market. Such advantages, however,
are offset to some extent by unfamiliarity with local consumption habits, cultural traits and by the difficulties
"outsiders", in contrast to "insiders", normally experience
when adjusting to the formal and informal web of the decision-making mechanism in the host country.

3.3.3. Oligopolistic product market constellation

Most markets for manufactured goods in present-day developed
economies conform to an oligopolistic model, in the sense
that the market supply is dominated by a few large companies
which devise their strategies in the light of the actual or
anticipated moves of their rivals. Firms strive to establish
a lead over their competitors by developing a new product,
brand or a cheaper production technique. However, a given
lead, once obtained, tends to be transient or vulnerable to
strong challenges by competitors. Competition among oli-
gopolists is therefore often fierce, indeed. Another

conceivable outcome of oligopolistic policies consists of the elimination or alleviation of competition by (generally convert) collusion among rivals. Considering their frequently significant strength vis-à-vis local producers, oligopolistic firms that have penetrated LDC markets (by way of local production or export sales from the home basis) may approximate a monopoly position. Heavy protection by the host country that benefits the first entrant would facilitate such an outcome. On the other hand, there is ample evidence that in many sectors and in countries with fairly sizeable market potential, in order to preserve a share of the market or to get a change of capturing part of it,   one MNE imitates the already established leader. (9)

3.3.4. Foreign Direct Investment as a "package" of Resources

In the neo-classical tradition, foreign direct investments were viewed as close analogues to portfolio investments. Nowadays, following the critique of S.Hymer in his seminal doctoral thesis, direct investments are conceived as representing the transfer of a "package" of resources. Although the transfer of funds remains the basic criterion underlying the statistical measurement of FDI, the non-financial ingredients of that package - and more particularly the technical "know-how", marketing and/or management - may be the more valuable resources to the MNE,   since they underpin market power, but also to the host country, intent upon improving its technological endownments. (10)

3.3.5. "Congenital ambivalence" of the subsidiaries

Affiliates in host countries are in a "congenitally ambivalent" position. (11) Subsidiaries are legal entities incorporated in the host country. Profits are normally earned in the local currency and balance sheets denominated in it. In many other respects the affiliate is firmly linked to the host country. Its fixed assets are located there and thus become possible targets of expropriation. The affiliates are subject to the local legislation and regulations which a sovereign state enforces on business enterprises within its borders. Not uncommonly, subsidiaries of foreign MNE's may even be discriminated against and subject to restrictions from which domestic firms are exempted. The exposure of the MNE, through its affiliates, to a number of alien and differing jurisdictions and cultures is indeed almost certainly the most essential feature of the MNE. But, at the same time, the local affiliate, especially when it is part of a set of interrelated companies or units, draws its inspiration and owes its very existence to a parent company located in a distant country. Even in the quite frequent loosely-controlled MNE, vital decisions such as those dealing with major extensions of productive capacity and market coverage tend to be decided at its main headquarters or, at a very minimum, require the latter's approval.

3.3.6. Internalization of transactions

The subsidiaries and the parent company are linked through
various internal financial flows. Even the loosely-controlled "holding company" type of MNE postulates some minimal financial links, such as dividend payments. Flows of commodities at various stages of processing occur between subsidiaries of vertically-integrated enterprises. As technical know-
how tends to be developed at headquarters and sustains the
subsidiaries, the latter are usually requested to contribute
to development costs. Such internal flows, which are substantial in a number of MBE, also create scope for manoeuvers
aiming at minimizing overall tax or other regulatory burdens.
It seems that the "transfer pricing" of these internal flows
may substantially deviate from those that would apply to un-
affiliated parties dealing "at arm's length" in an "open"
market. (12)

3.3.7. Objective functions of the Firm

The modern theory of the firm no longer views the profit-
maximization and a-temporal model of classical economics as
an adequate reflection of the aims of large businesses. Obviously, while a positive profit level remains a necessary
condition, profit maximization is usually pursued on a lon-
ger-term basis, whereas the preservation and expansion of
market shares and sheer survival are considered as prevailing
objectives of businesses. (13)

3.4. AREAS OF TENSION BETWEEN MULTINATIONAL ENTERPRISES AND DEVELOPING COUNTRIES

Many indictments are made against MNE. Reuber's study, for
example, contains a one-page list of more than fifteen such
charges alleged to have external effects. Many amongst them,
however, are clearly trivial; others are partial, in the
sense that they draw attention to given adverse economic consequences without looking at the aggregate macro-set of interrelated impacts derived from operations of MNE's. Thus,
the frequent assertion that profit remittances from the host
countries in any given year exceeds the net inflow of capital may be arithmetically exact, but this cannot be construed
as an overall negative balance-of-payments effect, as it
overlooks the impact which FDI has on other items of the balance sheet, particularly on imports and exports. Other
charges are clearly tinged by ideological beliefs and preju-
dices. Many statements about the MNE - even widely held ge-
neralizations - are tenuously based upon isolated case materials and anecdotical evidence.Finally, a priori theori-
zing about the plausible consequences of FDI, under given assumptions, readily points to contrary conclusions,once the
assumptions are modified. As a matter of fact, Reuber's "list"
of conceivable drawbacks is matched by a tally of equally
conceivable external benefits. (14)

Hence, there is a great need to pierce through casual and superficial statements "in favour of" or "against" the MNE and
to search for more fundamental insights into the causes of
the uneasy relationships between MNE's and nations states,
particularly those in the Third World. In my view, the following five areas can be identified as major areas of disagreement between the two parties. In line with the purpose of
this paper, only those two causes of tension that appear to
be quite specifically related to LDC's will be analysed in
the subsequent two sections.

3.4.1. Alien ownership

The fact that a sizeable portion of domestic industry in the
manufacturing sector belongs to non-resident corporations and
that, at a minimum,the major decisions in the subsidiaries
are made at or controlled by the foreign parent company emerges as a major source of animosity in LDC's towards the MNE.
This is especially true in Latin America where such "extran-
jerisation" or "de-nationalisation" creates a strong local
perception of "alienation" and "dependence" upon foreign
corporations.

Admittedly, there are also developed countries where a large
portion of local industry belongs to foreign interests. Canada
is the outstanding case where this kind of alienation is indeed
strongly resented. As against this, in Belgium, although foreign interests control a fairly large part of industry,no
such widespread opposition appears to exist. (15) Yet, the
"alienation syndrome" may be viewed as highly typical for the
LDC. As a matter of fact, and contrary to the case in many
developed countries, there is no two-way matrix of FDI. While
many developed countries such as Sweden, Switzerland or Belgium contain both domestic parent companies and subsidiaries
of foreign MNE's, LDC's are overwhelmingly the recipients of
FDI. There is a marked asymmetry in the pattern of FDI between LDC's and developed economies which prompts me to view
the "foreign ownership" syndrome as a cause of tension, unique to the relationship between the MNE and the LDC.

3.4.2. Cosmopolitan versus nationalist outlook

4.5. Autonomous and national governments take measures to ma-
ximize their inhabitants'social welfare. To this effect, they
exercise far-reaching sovereign powers which are only tempe-
red by the obligations of inter-nation comity and collaboration,as expressed in treaty obligations. In principle, a given nation is not obliged to heed other countries' interests,
if these are perceived to be or actually do run counter to
its own.

The large MNE's, on the other hand, do have a cosmopolitan
and potentially world-wide outlook. The objectives of increasing their market penetration and expanding their profits
force them to explore and implement optimal ways of penetra-

ting foreign markets. Both on account of genuine business
considerations (i.e. transport costs, the need for additional
productive capacity, etc.) and because of government measures
(particularly tariffs imposed on imports by the host country)
the establishment of producing affiliates in foreign markets
has become for MNE's a favoured way of becoming involved in
foreign markets. In attempting to improve their competitive
position, they also look for the lowest-cost locations.

Although MNE's,like other business enterprises, may invoke
special favours from their governments, they dislike government intervention on the whole and express a clear preference
for free international trade. There are three reasons for
this. First, such freedom would allow them, in principle, to
optimize the allocation of their resources, essentially according to their own private viewpoints. Secondly, it would
also prevent them from becoming trapped in the conflicting
interests of two or more countries where the MNE has a stake.
Plans to divest in Country A for relocation in Country B,
for example, might tend to be welcomed in Country B but be
heavily criticized by labour unions and the government in
Country A. And, finally, by definition, government intervention restricts the degree of freedom of business to operate.

Admittedly, governmental policy in Third World countries
tends to display a more nationalist stance than in high-income, free-enterprise countries. International trade also
appears to be more constrained there. But even in developed
countries governments typically put their interests ahead of
the global interests of the MNE. Thus, governments are loath
to accept the closure of local subsidiaries and see them
transferred to other, lower-cost locations. Or they may formally oppose the take-over of a prominent local company by
foreign interests, whereas, under other circumstances, foreign MNE's would be invited to help restructure local industry. (16) However, I am inclined, although with some he-
sitation, to view tension between nationalistic and cosmopolitan outlooks as part and parcel of the relationship between
MNE's and all nation states and not as a specific feature of
the LDC vis-à-vis the MNE.

3.4.3. Flexibility and scope for bypassing government regu-
       lations

Operating in a multi-jurisdiction framework significantly
complicates the task of managing the MNE, because the latter
is confronted with an array of highly differentiated economic
policy variables in the countries in which it operates. Yet,
through its subsidiaries, the presence of the MNE in many
countries provides scope for flexibility in bypassing national regulations. Since financial resources are a highly mo-
bile resource, such opportunities are quite extensive in the
financial area. Thus, if Subsidiary A cannot obtain credits
locally as the result of stringent anti-inflationary measures, Subsidiary B in another country may be called upon to
borrow in its credit market and relend the funds to Subsi-

diary A. The high degree of internalisation of the flows of
real and financial resources significantly enhances the
scope of the MNE for bypassing government regulations,since
a given subsidiary may be instructed to subordinate its interests to those of the MNE as a whole. Both this flexibility and the fact that major decisions are taken at main headquarters abroad erode the autonomy of national economic policy.

The loss of autonomy inflicted on nation states by such
regulation-bypassing manoeuvres is not unique to LDC's. As
a matter of fact, because of the larger stock of FDI in developed economies, in absolute terms, and because of the
two-way direct investment flows, developed economies are relatively more subjected than LDC's to the destabilizing effects which MNE operations may have on government policies.

3.4.4. The division of the benefits from FDI

It is frequently asserted that MNE's, because of their superior market or negotiating powers, are in a position to obtain an excessive portion of the benefits flowing from FDI.
This statement may be somewhat exaggerated. First, sovereignty affords ample powers to governments,even those of small
countries. As already mentioned, governments can attach severe conditions to the entry or the operations of the MNE;
the threat of nationalization may be a potent stick to induce the MNE to provide the host country with a more favourable share of FDI benefits. Besides, FDI can be expected to
bring an absolute increase in local value added: in absolute
terms, the recipient country is likely to obtain more FDI benefits from a larger pie than if the FDI projects had not
been implemented, even assuming that the MNE is able to appropriate the lion's share of the value added.

At any rate, considering the conflicting objective functions of governments and LDC's the relative division of the
net benefits arising from FDI, in itself, becomes a matter
of contention. Governments seek to increase their share of
the pie and MNE's attempt to use their strong negotiating
cards or to construe actions and manoeuvers, which, while
not overtly violating existing laws, aim at minimizing governments' share. Recent literature, and especially the
writings of Vaitsos, stress the bargaining framework in which
the relationship between MNE's and government is cast. (17)

Judging from the literature and from events on the political level, the division-of-gains issue attracts manifestly
more attention in LDC's than in developed countries. This is
understandable since, as previously mentioned, LDC's are typically only recipients and not originators of FDI. But, in
high-income countries, the division of relative FDI benefits
is also a matter of concern. Thus, several capital-exporting
countries (especially the United States and Western Germany)
have taken action to preserve their part of the taxable base
when MNE's have attempted to channel taxable profits to
somewhat artificial subsidiaries in low-tax jurisdictions.

Besides, the measures which host countries enact regarding
the ownership of affiliates frequently aim largely at enhancing the country's share of FDI benefits. Hence, the divi-
sion-of-benefits issue is included to some extent in the ensuing discussion of the ownership syndrome. A more detailed
empirical analysis of the division of benefits between MNE's
and governments would go beyond the limits of this paper.
Its treatment, in macro-economic terms, also runs into serious conceptual and statistical problems. (18)

3.5. THE ALIENATION SYNDROME

3.5.1. Resentment

Ownership and the resulting control (albeit in varying degrees) of local affiliates by foreign enterprises emerge as
specific sources of tension between MNE's and LDC's. The
role of foreign MNE's in the local economy of a large number
of LDC's appears to be not only quite substantial but to also have grown during the 1960's, both in relative and absolute terms. (19) Beyond the actual degree of foreign participation in the domestic economy, the perception by the host
country of the acceptability of that foreign intrusion is
the basic factor in determining the degree of resentment
against FDI. The threshold of tolerance vis-à-vis foreign
intrusion obviously differs significantly from one country
to another and may display substantial shifts within the
same host country over a period of time.

The resentment, and its degree of virulence, is likely to
be fed by various real or alleged negative effects of inward
FDI on the host country. First, under otherwise equal circumstances, i.e. as compared to a situation where the same
firm would be owned by domestic interests and would be equally efficient, foreign ownership results in the outflow of a
portion of value added in the form of profits and profit-like
remittances (such as licensing fees, service charges), thus
negatively affecting the balance of payments. Second, the
control exercised by the parent companies may thwart the conduct of domestic economic policies. As already mentioned,
however, this effect is not limited to LDC's, but is also a
cause of concern for governments of developed countries. Furthermore, on a more fundamental political level, foreign presence, when it is viewed as excessive, is resented as an in-
tolerable erosion of national sovereignty and of the host
country's ability to control its own economic affairs.

And finally, foreign-owned ventures may be utterly unacceptable on ideological grounds to LDC's, when, for example,
the latter have adopted a Marxist pattern of society, which in
principle bans private property.

In LDC's nationalistic feelings tend to be strong. Most
presentday LDC's were until recently colonies of Western powers. Memories of the lack of self-determination, and of hu-
miliation, still linger. Besides, elites in LDC's view natio-

nalist loyalties as a powerful catalyst in integrating the
nation-state when strong regional or tribal centrifugal tendencies are present.
    Nationalism is a rather elusive concept. It can be discus-
sed in terms of both its negative and positive aspects. On
the negative side, there is a feeling of exclusiveness, i.e.
the sentiment that other nations or groups are different, do
not belong and should not be admitted to one's own society.
Hence, a tendency to display aloofness towards foreigners
and alien elements exists, whereby foreign elements may be
rejected, purely on account of their foreignness. Adversities
tend to be blamed by governments or public opinion on foreigners. On the positive side, nationalism stresses the dis-
tinct personality and interests of the own nation. As Vaitsos
has noted, nationalist feelings and attitudes, particularly
in Latin America, emphasize deliberate action for fuller employment and qualitative upgrading of both human and physical
domestic resources, so such feelings may perform a more active and commanding role in economic development. (20)
    Resentment against foreign ownership is particularly
strong with respect to take-overs of existing firms -- apparently a predominant way of entering the host-country markets. (21) Criticism of foreign take-overs is quite understandable since they imply a substitution of existing domes-
tically-owned firms by foreign-controlled ventures, whereas
investments in new industries would result in additions to
the existing stock of productive capacity.

3.5.2. Ownership-restricting measures

As mentioned at the outset of this paper, LDC's on the whole,
tend to apply a stringent spectrum of controls on incoming
and on already established foreign ventures. A number of
these restrictive measures aim at reducing the extent of foreign ownership within the local economy. The principal types
of controls are:
- prohibitions on the entry of MNE into key sectors such as
  telecommunications, public utilities, and banking. (One
  should add that in developed economies, especially in Europe, such sectors frequently belong to the public sector
  or are strictly controlled by government).
- nationalization of existing affiliates by the government of
  the host country. In recent years, the pace of these nationalizations has been accelerating, not only in the mineral
  sector but also in the manufacturing sector. (22)
- prohibition of wholly-owned subsidiaries. Except in special
  cases and under strict conditions, e.g. a satisfactory export performance, only joint ventures with domestic partners belonging to the public and/or the private sector and
  commanding a majority position are permissible. India provides a prominent example of such a policy.
- divestment rules whereby the extent of foreign ownership of
  local subsidiaries is reduced. Thus, in some countries, foreign interests have been forced to relinquish full or ma-

jority ownership. The famous "resolution 24" of the Andean Pact countries subjects foreign ventures to a progressive process of divestment and transfer of share ownership to domestic interests.
- technology transfer, an alternative road to foreign direct investment,which appears to be catching on in various countries and has found strong advocates in the economic literature. (23) Instead of acquiring the package of resources which is inherent in the FDI act, LDC's may prefer to break it up and obtain the various ingredients individually. Thus, technology may be purchased via a licensing contract. This has been the preferred approach in Japan and one which obviously has been quite successful in promoting that country to one of the highest levels of technological proficiency. There exists a market, albeit an imperfect one, for such resources. Other, non-proprietary resources (i.e. those not protected by patents), such as management expertise may also be bought or hired. The ingredients acquired in this way are then combined with already available resources or obtained from other firms. The transfer of resources no longer occurs within and through a subsidiary,which is fully or partially owned by a foreign MNE.

The detailed conditions of technology transfer greatly vary. Through it, the LDC obtains technical and managerial resources by piecemeal purchases and without resultant foreign ownership of the production unit. A trend towards increased technology-transfer activity has been noted in recent years. (24)
  A full analysis of the determinants of technology transfer would require a highly-involved study and is probably not possible at the present stage of available data. Yet, some useful comments may be ventured about the main factors which strengthen or weaken the negotiating powers of governments vis-à-vis MNE's. The underlying assumption is that LDC's view as less desirable a situation where local subsidiaries are exclusively or substantially owned by foreign interests. In their view, the "first-best" arrangement would consist in either the selective acquisition of the needed resources or by way of technology transfer. LDC's must take into consideration the fact that, on the whole, MNE's have a preference for wholly-owned subsidiaries, which allows them stricter control over their operations. By maintaining an internalized flow of resource, ownership permits MNE's to protect the knowledge factor on which the firm's leading position may depend rather than risk having it divulged to and appropriated by competitors.

3.5.3. Trump Cards of Developing Countries

The following factors can easily be identified as enhancing the bargaining power of the LDC vis-à-vis the MNE:
- local markets: as already intimated, LDC's with a comparatively large market potential have much more to offer to

MNE's than small countries at a low level of development.
The attractive size of the market results from a per capita
income well above subsistence levels (say, above the $ 500
line) and/or large populations. This consideration, however, applies only for FDI that is geared to the local market potential and not that of the export-oriented type,
where low-labour-cost countries are used as platforms for
the export of labour-intensive finished goods or components.
- rich mineral resources such as oil and phosphate may, in
given circumstances, become a strong card for the LDC's.
High world demand and a monopoly position would allow LDC's
to drive up prices and to appropriate the lion's share of
the locational rent which low production-cost endowments
of natural resources afford. Furthermore, MNE's may be willing to accept a comparatively high price against the assurance of uninterrupted supplies of raw material. The usually
highly homogeneous character of mineral resources, however,
enhances the competition among the LDC's supplying the same
raw materials - unless they band together in a tight cartel
such as OPEC.
- even in small countries, the impact of national sovereignty
is very comprehensive; a sovereign nation can exercise legal powers which, in principle, are unrestricted. The only
limitations stem from (a) international agreements (including some unwritten, vague rules of international public
law to which the LDC has voluntarily subscribed); (b) the
physical impossibility of implementing measures outside its
own territory; and (c) actual or potential retaliation by
foreign powers. Gunboat diplomacy, however, now belongs to
a previous age. As A.Emmanuel notes, even small LDC's have
expropriated the affiliates of giant MNE's. (25) To some extent the assets of the MNE in a 'host' country are thus
liable to becoming 'hostages'.
- As H.Johnson has stressed, the "knowledge ingredients" from
which the MNE's derive their often superior technology and
management, have a high opportunity cost and, hence, a high
value for the recipient LDC. It allows the LDC to avail itself of modern technology without having to incur the high
costs and risks which separate autarchic development of the
same technology would entail. To the MNE, however, the marginal cost of spreading and using the knowledge, once produced and amortized, becomes minimal. (26) Because of the
low additional cost of transferring the knowledge resources, the MNE may be willing to accept a lower fee for the
transfer when faced by a strong negotiating posture on the
part of the LDC.
- Finally, when it wants to attract a given type of investment, the LDC with substantial market potential usually
does not face a monopolist MNE. More typically, several
large MNE's, strongly competing amongst each other in oligopolistic product markets, are interested in entering the
host country markets. The market for FDI then becomes not
one of bilateral monopoly but rather of monopsony with one
demanding LDC facing a number of MNE. Thus, the LDC is in
a position to play off one MNE against others and to choose

the comparatively most favorable offer. In several industries - e.g. the oil sector - the relative position of the
traditionally leading firms has been significantly eroded
by the entry of "minors" or "outsiders" into the arena of
international business. (27)

3.5.4. Limitations to the Bargaining Powers of Developing Countries

The scope for tough bargaining by the LDC is nonetheless seriously constrained by various factors. If the conditions
imposed by the host country become excessive, the MNE may no
longer be willing to provide the resources requested.Although
LDC's tend to view the contribution of MNE's to their welfare
as inversely related to the extent of foreign ownership, the
real effects of alternative ownership patterns may not bear
out that assumption. Technology transmitted through joint
ventures or licensing agreements may not be the most up-to-
date, or they may soon be superseded by new advances by the
same or other MNE's. Some of the ingredients of superior
knowledge, such as management, may more efficiently coalesce
with the other resources needed when that component remains
imbedded in the 100 percent-owned full package. (28) Thus India in 1977 could enforce upon Coca-Cola the option either to
divulge the production secret of its glamorous, branded beverage or leave the Indian market altogether, because it had do-
mestically evolved a somewhat similar beverage which can be
marketed behind protective barriers. In countries with an already comprehensive industrial base such as Brazil and India,
domestic entrepreneurs are available as substitutes for 100
percent FDI. They, generally and understandably, oppose the
intrusion of foreign MNE's into their local market, except to
the extent that various forms of collaboration may be expected to strengthen their own position. Hence, they tend to act
in a nationalistic way.
  MNE's usually manufacture capital goods or fairly sophisticated consumer goods; they are much less involved in simple
consumer goods like textiles. This explains why, apart from
Socialist countries, the tendency towards technology transfer
and the rollback of the 100 percent ownership pattern is more
noticeable in countries, such as India or Brazil, where industrialization has progressed to the stage where high-tech-
nology products are becoming a significant element of the industrial scene and in which local entrepreneurship and knowledge resources can substitute for some of the resources
which the "package" of wholly-owned FDI contains.
  It is worth noticing, however, that even if the packaged
form were to yield more net benefits to the recipient country,
the latter may still prefer to obtain resources separately.
The "depackaged" approach yields a more satisfactory level of
enjoyment of a highly-valued collective public good, viz. autonomy and the ability to make one's own decisions. Political
viewpoints, then, take precedence over economic considerations.

On a more general level, one must add that when the LDC has
appropriated formal ownership of and control over the local
subsidiaries it may fall substantially short of real command
over the strategies and operations of that subsidiary. The
host country can only control the affiliate located within
its borders, and the affiliate's efficiency often depends on
the operations abroad of other subsidiaries of the same MNE.
Besides, other functions in the production process, especially downstream ones such as marketing and transport, may remain
under the control of the same MNE or of other foreign firms.
(29)

3.6. THE PRODUCT-MIX OF MULTINATIONAL ENTERPRISES

3.6.1. The Issue

In recent years, a new argument against MNE's has been voiced
with increasing forcefulness. It is claimed that both the
range of products of MNE's and their production processes are
not appropriate to the "real" needs of LDC's. The output of
MNE's in the manufacturing sector, for example, largely consists of fairly sophisticated products. Characterized by a
high income elasticity of demand, they appeal to the better-
off classes in the Third World,with purchasing power adequate
to adoption of "Northern" high-income patterns of consumption. Large segments of the population, who may labour under
dire, "absolute" poverty, do not get any appreciable benefit
out of such operations of MNE's. In their production processes MNE's are also alleged to use comparatively high capital-
intensive methods of production in the LDC, while the factor
endowment of these countries calls for the use of more labour-intensive processes.
    The issue thus raised obviously relates only to LDC's and
requires somewhat more detailed treatment. This topic has
come to the fore in a new approach to development which is
apparently rapidly gaining adherents, and which makes the
eradication of the absolute poverty of large segments of the
population in the Third World a priority objective of national development strategies and of cooperative action on the
international level.
    This critique against MNE's can only be approached within
a normative framework of analysis, whereby the strategy of
economic development recommended is one which gives priority
to satisfaction of the needs of the poorest strata of LDC
societies. Such a strategy is strongly advocated by several
international agencies including the World Bank and the International Labour Office. I intend to outline this "basic
needs" approach and to briefly examine what role the MNE
could conceivably perform in its implementation. I will assume that present MNE involvement in LDC's is not conducive
to satisfying the needs of the poor masses; their exists ample empirical evidence to support this contention. I shall
selectively focus on the "product mix" of MNE's, to the ex-

clusion of their role as providers of employment opportunities. A related charge which, because of its specialized character I do not cover in this paper, states that the relatively capital-intensive production processes of MNE's are unsuited to the factor endowments of LDC's.

3.6.2. The Basic-Needs Approach

The International Labour Office specifies the contents of the basic needs approach as follows: "First, minimum requirements of a family for items of private consumption. Adequate food, shelter and clothing obviously are included, as are household implements and furniture: and depending on the average income of the society, other goods and services might be added. Second, basic needs include essential services provided by the community at large, e.g. safe drinking water, sanitation facilities, public transport, health and educational facilities. None of these things can be supplied unless there is adequate employment. ... Thus productive and adequately remunerated employment is a basic need in itself... Closely related to basic needs, but separate, is the wish of people to participate in making the decisions which affect their lives". (30)
    Thus, the basic-needs approach is multidimensional and aims at tackling various aspects of poverty simultaneously. The fundamental aim of the basic-needs strategy appears to be eradication of sub-human levels of living. Although the target level of income that would allow basic needs to be satisfied is not at all ambitious and, for example, would not exceed $ 50 for the "destitute" in Asia and $ 100 for the "seriously poor", the numbers belonging to these categories are staggering; according to one estimate, the "destitute" would represent 42 percent of the population in Asia, 39 percent in Africa and 27 percent in Latin America. (31) Those segments of the populations, situated in the lowest levels of the income-distribution pyramid, are identified as "target groups" or as priority beneficiaries of the new strategy. They are found in the "informal" urban sector (mostly living in squalid "bidonvilles") and among the much more numerous groups of peasants, tenants and landless labourers in the vast rural sector.
    It is apparently also postulated that, as a result of the successful implementation of the basic-needs approach, the relative income position of the lowest income strata - as expressed, for example, in terms of the spread between the lowest and the highest income deciles - would improve. Presumably, it is hoped that improvement of the appalling position of the absolute poor should and could be accompanied by rapid growth in the traditional sense, i.e. with a fast increase in GDP and per capita income. As a matter of fact, the scope for improving the relative status of the poor by "statically" redistributing existing incomes and assets is limited. This is because of the small number of rich people and the large masses of absolute poor. (32)

The basic-needs approach deserves approval on ethical, political, social and economic grounds. A state of affairs in which the happy few can indulge in conspicuous consumption amid the masses of the population who barely survive in misery and desolation is morally revolting. A society and a growth pattern which leave large segments of the population in dire misery cannot be called optimal even if the number of the comparatively well-to-do grows rapidly and the so-called middle classes expand. Stark contrasts in wealth and well-being are apt to provoke social unrest. In economic terms, qualms about the theoretical non-comparability of individual welfare functions cannot overrule the economic principle that the first hundred dollars of the poor man have more marginal utility for the individual concerned, and for society at large, than the excess hundred dollars of the rich man.

Admittedly, implementation of the basic-needs approach, while eminently advisable, is bound to run into serious difficulties. It poses stubborn technical problems in terms of the optimal combination of its multi-faceted ingredients. Deeply-engrained societal inertia must also be overcome. Excessive emphasis on the social redistributive aspects, to the detriment of indispensable productivity-enhancing measures would, in a poor country, become counterproductive to the very aims of the strategy. The large budgetary requirements for the physical and social infrastructure needed to implement the basic-needs projects preclude an immediate comprehensive coverage of regions and population segments. Implementation in the field calls for the efficient use of well-motivated extension workers who would be able, hopefully, to induce the target groups concerned into a self-help mentality and attitudes. And perhaps above all, political commitment to a policy which implies profound shifts in priorities and in the use of instruments as compared to traditional policies with their bias in favour of urban classes and of industrial expansion must be forthcoming. The new strategy calls for a profound reorientation of the sectorial and regional allocation of public investments, for a shift in the intersectoral terms of trade (which are usually stacked against agriculture) and, most critically, for a change in the asset structure through land reform.

These various constraints are indeed formidable. If unattended, they carry the risk that the new strategy may not fare any better than the many preceding formulae for rapid development (such as planning, the green revolution, birth control), the excessive hopes for which were only too soon greatly dashed. In my discussion of the role which MNE's actually perform or could conceivable play within the framework of a basic-needs strategy, I shall nonetheless assume that the strategy is capable of being efficiently implemented. This assumption finds support in a preliminary assessment of the large number of integrated rural development projects initiated by the World Bank which concludes that "the start is promising but the problems are formidable". (33)

3.6.3. A Digression on "Basic-Needs Goods"

The basic-needs approach would require the poorest strata of the population to be supplied with sufficient cheap and necessary (or at least highly-useful) goods and services, so they are able to enjoy a modest but decent level of living, capable of satisfying their most essential needs. Such basic goods and services should be available at prices the poorest people can afford. Among the goods that satisfy fundamental needs, one should mention, first of all, adequate and diversified food, which is the largest item in the average budget in low-income countries and the overriding preoccupation of the poorest strata of the population. (34) Other essential needs relate to a modest array of clothing, some furniture and kitchen utensils, and a simple dwelling available at a low rent. Needless-to-say, the ability of the poor to afford such goods and to become integrated in the monetized sector depends on the stability and the level of their incomes. Such improvement is only realistically sustainable by expanding the opportunities for productive employment. Accordingly the letter must become a priority objective of government policies.

Although the situation of the poorest target groups deserves priority attention, it would be excessive and counterproductive to cast the definition of "basic-needs" in almost physiological terms and in a static fashion. There are a number of highly useful and intensely coveted goods, standard perquisites in lower middle-income families in rich countries, which households in low-income countries also want and for which they are willing to work and spend their savings. Among such "incentive goods" one may mention radios, sewing machines, bicycles and watches. (35) One should add that several such categories of goods enhance productivity, as for example, simple implements used in agriculture. A policy which would exclusively cater to the poorest strata would carry the risk of hindering the improvement of welfare of large segments of the population which, while distinctly better-off than the destitute, are still living in quite modest conditions. In any case, such an extreme anti-poverty policy would be politically unpalatable.

From the above definition of "basic-needs", it follows that the other main category of "basic-needs goods and services" consists of public goods and services supplying educational and health facilities. Public health must be viewed in a broad sense to include safe drinking water, sewage disposal systems and other similar facilities. The poorer groups of the population should have access to such services at no or at very low cost. Admittedly, because of the obvious budgetary implications of large-scale public programs, such services will often be but minimal.

3.6.4. The actual product mix of MNE's

The product mix of MNE's obviously stretches over a very

wide spectrum of goods and services. Several sectors in
which they operate are not directly relevant to our enquiry.
Thus, mineral production and export-oriented projects are
geared to outlets in foreign markets. In the larger LDC's,
MNE's are frequently involved in the manufacture of intermediate goods like heavy chemicals, fertilizers or machines.
Whether such production units are satisfying the demand of
the upper classes instead of that of the poorer ones would
ultimately depend on the type of end product for which they
serve as inputs. This leaves for our attention both durable
and non-durable consumption goods.

It appears fair to state that MNE's are mainly manufacturing goods in LDC's that are not satisfying basic-needs but
appeal primarily to the higher-income classes. (36) There
are obviously significant exceptions such as some durable
consumer goods (such as radios), which have reached the stage
of low-cost standardized production and come within reach of
wide strata of the population. They are a typical example of
the so-called incentive goods.

3.6.5. A Problem of Attribution

If we accept the general proposition that the product mix of
MNE's is biased against satisfying the needs of the poorest
strata of the population, it follows that if a basic-needs
policy approach is to be pursued with vigor,the role of the
MNE should be drastically curtailed or at least redirected.
Before dealing with this normative aspect, a few comments
appear in order to avoid unwarranted or unrealistic inferen-
ces being drawn. First, the impact which a Western-style
consumption pattern exerts on LDC's cannot be attributed so-
lely to multinational firms, i.e. to production by foreign
firms within the LDC's themselves. As a matter of fact, import of more "modern" sophisticated goods from the higher-
income countries is an alternative, and frequently the first
channel through which Western higher-income consumption
goods are "demonstrated" in LDC's. (37)

Second, the seduction which higher-income consumption
patterns and commodities exert on large segments of the population of low-income countries should be viewed as one aspect of the broader dialectical process between tradition
and modernization. The tremendous economic growth which began gathering momentum in 18th century Western Europe has
dramatically modified and modernized both the economic scene
and the mentality of that part of the world. At later stages, it affected other countries in which Western commodities or life-styles were introduced, most often in the wake
of colonial conquest. While higher living standards should
not be equated with greater "happiness" - which transcends
economic categories - the upgrading of the level of material
well-being is rightly regarded as a desirable and uncontro-
vertible objective in modern societies.

Hence, the attraction of commodities associated with
higher standards of living on large groups in poor countries

is, to quite an extent, unavoidable. Even "Iron Curtains" cannot completely shield LDC's from such influences. The improvement of consumption levels and the acquisition of many of the amenities of modern life naturally correspond to a keenly-felt desire of human beings. Higher consumption levels also give tangible proof of economic progress. Even governments bent on a rapid industrialization and a high rate of accumulation cannot indefinitely deny the widespread urge to consume more and better-quality goods.

Finally, the advent of modern industry and living patterns is bound to have some destabilizing effects on the value systems of traditional societies. Thus, the surge of mechanized industry has a devastating impact on low-productivity handicraft modes of production, irrespective of whether the machines are introduced by foreign or domestic firms. The relative shift from agricultural to industrial employment brings about an increasingly urban-centered way of living and civilization. The attractions of modern amenities exacerbate the exodus from rural areas to chaotically-growing cities.

The onslaught of modernization on traditional societies understandably provokes tensions and opposition of various types, especially when Western values intrude upon non-Western cultures. Groups that are threatened in their traditional cultural value-systems or in their economic interests will react in a hostile way vis-à-vis alien elements and seek to preserve their own heritage. Other groups are more open to foreign influences in the belief that only the adoption of Western methods and values opens the way to modernization. And yet, change is the unescapable destiny of societies in the modern world. Change unavoidably entails some pain and destabilizing effects. The history of most LDC's - and of Western Europe in earlier days as well - illustrates the clash of old and new values, ideas and attitudes. (38)

One may conclude that it would be a gross oversimplification to attribute the pervasiveness and persistence of absolute poverty in the LDC's to the operations of the MNE's. The product mix of MNE's is only one aspect of a wider phenomenon in which commodities of affluent societies are being demonstrated and transplanted into low-income countries. Besides, as stressed above, the operation of production units within the LDC's, or the process of multinationalisation proper, is not a necessary condition to such transference - although, for our purposes, it is rather immaterial whether LDC markets are covered through exports from the home base or through local affiliates in LDC's, as these two functions tend to be performed by the same MNE's. Second, although MNE's, like other firms and entities, may attempt to influence government policies, much of the neglect of the poorest strata of the population and of the agricultural sector must be blamed primarily on the faulty or insufficiently balanced policies of sovereign governments.

The fundamental message which the basic-needs strategy contains is not that non-essential goods or even luxury goods are by definition contemptable but that, on account of the intolerably wide spread of absolute poverty in most LDC's and

on account of the gap in their well-being with better-to-do
classes, the improvement (in absolute and relative terms) of
the position of the poorest classes should become a primary
goal of economic strategy and policies.

3.6.6. Possible Role of Multinational Enterprises in a Basic-Needs Approach

Let us accept the argument that, in the light of a "basic-
needs" strategy, the operations of MNE's should be geared
more to commodities that cater to the fundamental needs of
the lower strata of the population. The question for discussion, then, is whether MNE's can be induced to alter their
output-mix so as to be more in line with the limited purchasing power and the priority needs of the poorest segments of
the population in poor countries.

From a technical viewpoint, MNE's could undertake mass-
produced "basic-needs commodities" without difficulties. They
have pioneered new products for mass consumption - although
the mass spread among the consumers usually only occurred at
a later stage, further cost-reducing technological progress
and higher per capita income levels permitting. Some MNE's
also posses an extensive distribution network that stretches
deeply into the countryside. For example, this is the case
for Unilever in India. (39) Its highly efficient production
processes also usually allow for higher quality and hygienic
standards than local production can ensure.

In economic terms, however, MNE's appear on the whole less
suited to the manufacture of "basic-needs goods". Admittedly,
a modern sector manufacturing firm could undertake a profitable business in the production of basic-needs goods if large
turnover and mass production were to compensate for the small
profit margins on low-priced commodities. But there are several circumstances which discourage MNE's from moving into
production of basic-needs goods for mass consumption by the
poor, and the wisdom of inducing MNE's to move into such
fields is highly questionable. First, even mass-produced "basic-needs goods" easily become too expensive. The agri-business sector may serve as an example of this. Alan Berg mentions "incaparina", a high-protein food of excellent quality
marketed in Central America, which proved too expensive compared to more traditional maize staple-products. (40) Even at
very low profit margins, the production costs and those of
standarized packaging and transport rendered incaparina too
costly, when compared to the cost of local foods. This and
other examples in the agri-business field show that trans-
plantation of modern ("Western") food products and the methods used to market them in poor societies may become socially unproductive.

Another factor argues against an extensive role of MNE's
in the supply of "basic-needs goods". Most of these commodities are quite simple; they can and should be produced locally. This is obvious as far as dairy foods are concerned, and
many household utensils and simple agricultural implements

are traditionally supplied by domestic handicrafts. Although
the chances for survival of those handicrafts in the face of
the more mechanical production processes is doubtful in the
longer run, it would clearly be socially objectionable to
prompt MNE's to enter these fields. For several of the comparatively simple standardized "incentive goods" mentioned
above, e.g. bicycles, sewing machines or clothes, local enterprises are also readily available once a country gets moving toward industrialization.

In fact, one should not expect MNE's to take the initiative of entering the "basic-needs" sector for <u>direct</u> production to consumers on a sizeable scale. Their real strengths
lie elsewhere. Their high level of technology, the rapid pace
of product innovation and their capital-intensive production
function ensure a strong position in the origination and mar-
kering of goods destined to upper- and middle-class budgets.
(41)

Yet, MNE's can make a valuable contribution towards solving the problems of the destitute and the poor by harnessing
their technological proficiency for the benefit of projects
catering to the target groups of the poorest people. Simple
housing, irrigation pumps, basic medicines, high-yielding
seed varieties, mass media for the dissemination of educational services (by satellite) are examples that readily come to
mind. The point to make here is that MNE's cannot be expected
to sell such goods <u>directly</u> to individual poor peasants or
shanty-town dwellers, as these lack adequate purchasing power.
The new products, equipment and production methods suited to
LDC's which MNE's are able to develop can be inserted into
government-directed projects, which primarily aim at overcoming absolute poverty. Thus, poverty groups may benefit <u>indi-
rectly</u> from MNE endeavors.

3.7. CONCLUDING REMARKS

In this paper, an attempt was made to identify and to briefly
discuss some indictments which are frequently made against
MNE's in LDC's and which appear to be specific in the sense
that they relate <u>both</u> to the <u>multinational</u> dimension of modern business and to the conditions of LDC's with <u>low per capita levels</u> and widespread absolute poverty. Upon closer in-
spection, the causes of tension, which I deem to be specific
to the relationship between LDC's and MNE's can be linked to
the broader economic and non-economic impact which the patterns of production and consumption in high-income countries
are bound to exert on low-income LDC's. That impact itself
results from the basically unequal and asymmatrical position
of high- and low-income countries. Typically, MNE's are located in the former and their new products are transmitted from
the home-country base to foreign markets. When a normative
view is taken and the needs of the poorest segments of the
population in LDC's are rightly given priority, the output-
mix of MNE's appears less suited to LDC's.

FOOTNOTES

1. See Whichard, O., "US Direct Investment Abroad in 1976", Survey of Current Business, Augustus 1977.

2. Reuber, G. and associates, Private Foreign Investment in Development, Oxford University Press, 1973, p.4.

3. Dunning, J. and Gilman, M., "Alternative Policy Prescriptions and the Multinational Enterprise", in The Multinational Enterprise in a Hostile World, ed. by Curzon, and Curzon, V, Macmillan, 1977, p.36.

4. As shown in the evidence discussed in Bethke, V. and Koopmann, G., Multinationale Unternehmen und Entwicklungsländer. Interessenkonflikte und Verhandlungspositionen, Verlag Weltarchiv, Hamburg, 1975.

5. For empirical work on the relationship between the structure of industry and per capita income levels, see various writings of Chenery, H.

6. See Chenery, H. and associates, Redistribution with Growth, Oxford University Press, 1974. An influential book in drawing attention to the absolute dimensions of poverty and in advocating a development strategy which focuses on the satisfaction of "basic-needs".

7. As the term has been coined in the sociographic study of Lewis, O., The Children of Sanchez, Penguin Series, 1961.

8. For a perceptive and well-documented discussion of the clash between (modern) "Western" and traditional "Eastern" values, see Myrdal, G., Asian Drama, An Enquiry into the Poverty of Nations, Twentieth Century Fund, Penguin Books, 1968, Volume I, chapters II and III.

9. The follow-the-leader gambit emerges clearly in Knickerbocker, F., Oligopolistic Reaction and the Multinational Enterprise, Harvard University Press, 1973.

10. Hymer, S., The International Operations of National Forms: A Study of Direct Foreign Investment, M.I.T. Press, 1976. The "package" concept is also stressed by Vaitsos, C., in various writings.

11. Plasschaert, S., "L'ambivalence congénitale des entreprises multinationales", Revue de la société d'études et d'expansion, July-August-September 1974.

12. Internalization is viewed as a significant determinant of the multinalization process of firms in Buckley, P.

and Casson, M., The Future of the Multinational Enterprise, Macmillan, London, 1976.

13. For a brief survey, see The Modern Business Enterprise. Selected Readings, Penguin Books, 1972 and especially the "Introduction" by the editor Gilbert, M..

14. Reuber, G.L. and associates, cit., p.20-21.

15. Van Den Bulcke, D., De Multinationale Onderneming. Een Typologische Benadering, SERUG, Ghent, 1975, passim.

16. For interesting cases in France, see Bertin, G., "Industrial Policy and the Structural Impact of Multinational Firms. An Analytical View", in ed. Jacquemin, A. and De Jong, H., Markets, Corporate Behaviour and the State, Nijenrode Series, 1976.

17. See especially Vaitsos, C., Intercountry Income Distribution and Transnational Enterprises, Clarendon Press, Oxford, 1974.

18. For a brief discussion of the methodological issues involved, see Dunning, J., "Evaluating the Costs and Benefits of FDI: Some General Observations", University of Reading Department of Economics Discussion Papers in International Investment and Business Studies, nr.37, 1977, section II and III.

19. As suggested by partial data assembled in table B of Vernon, R., Storm over the Multinationals. The Real Issues, Harvard University Press, 1977, p.78.

20. Vaitsos, C.V., "Policies on Foreign Direct Investment and Economic Development in Latin America", IDS Communication, n.106, University of Sussex, 1974.

21. A tally mentioned in Vernon, R. in Multinational Enterprises in Developing Countries: an Analysis of National and National Policies, Harvard Institute for International Development, Development Discussion Paper, n.4, 1975, p.23 shows that 56.9 percent of foreign-based ventures by both non-American and American MNE's had resulted from take-overs of existing firms. The data pertain to 1970 and 1968, respectively.

22. The United Nations counted 875 cases of nationalizations or take-overs in the 1960 to mid 1974 period in 62 different countries. Mentioned by Vaitsos, C.V., "Power, Knowledge and Development Policy: Relations between transnational enterprises and developing countries" in ed. Helleiner, G.K., A World Divided. The Less Developed Countries in the International Economy, Cambridge University Press, 1976, p.129.

23. See Vaitsos, C.V., in several of his writings and more particularly in his Sussex paper, mentioned in note (20).

24. See Vaitsos, C.V. in his Sussex paper.

25. Emmanuel, A., Interprétation des activités des sociétés transnationales donnée suivant les différentes théories actuelles du développement, paper submitted to a UNESCO conference 1976, mimeographed, p.29.

26. Johnson, H.G., "The Efficiency and Welfare Implications of the International Corporation", in Kindleberger, C.P. ed. The International Corporation, MIT Press, 1970; reprinted in International Investment, ed. Dunning, J., Penguin Series, 1972.

27. See the graph in Vernon, R., Storm over the Multinationals, cit., p.81, which shows a declining degree of concentration in the worldwide production of eight commodities; and Usui, M., "Transnational Enterprises and International Development: A New Focus in the Perspective of Industrial and Technological Cooperation" in Transfer of Technology by Multinational Corporations, OECD, 1977.

28. As argued by Usui, M., in Oligopoly, R and D and Licensing -- A Reflection Towards a Fair Deal in Technology Transfer, OECD Development Centre, Occasional Paper, n.7.

29. As stressed by Penrose, E.T. in "The Growth of International Corporations and their Changing Role in Under-Developed Countries", in La Croissance de la Grande Firme Multinationale, ed. Bertin, G., Centre National de la recherche scientifique, Paris, 1973.

30. Cited from the more succinct draft. The final text is in Employment, Growth and Basic Needs, International Labour Office, Geneva, 1976, p.32.

31. Ibid., p.20-25.

32. Thus, in India, according to Minhas, B., "Rural Poverty, Land Redistribution and Economic Strategy", Indian Econo-Review, April 1970, p.97-128. a fairly radical redistribution of land would only save 7 percent of the rural population from absolute poverty.
    Besides, in an excellent article, Stewart, F. and Streeten, P. draw attention to conceptual ambiguities and to variations which the new approach may contain. See, New Strategies for Development, Poverty, Income Distribution, and Growth, Oxford Economic Papers, November 1976.

33. See the article, under the same title, in Report - News of the World Bank, September-October 1977.

34. As Engle's law leads us to expect. For evidence, see Kra-

vis, I. and associates, <u>A System of International Compa-</u>
<u>risons of Gross Product and Purchasing Power</u>, John Hop-
kins University Press, 1975, especially p.242-3, table
14.II.

35. Vice Premier Teng Hsiao-Ping of the People's Republic of
China is reported to have said recently that "each family
must have a bicycle, a sewing machine, a television set",
according to "Who's No.1?". in <u>Newsweek</u>, September 12,
1977. Such goals would appear feasible and desirable once
the most basic needs have been met and absolute poverty
eradicated, a performance which is generally ascribed to
the People's Republic of China.

36. This point is stressed in various writings of Streeten,
P.. For some interesting empirical evidence see Leontia-
des, J., <u>Patterns in International Markets and Market</u>
<u>Strategy</u>, mimeo, 1976.

37. The role of imports is stressed in Hirschman, A., <u>The</u>
<u>Strategy of Economic Development</u>, Yale University Press,
1958, passim.

38. Thus, the complex interaction between the push of one's
own (Indian) values and the pull of Western modernization
is admirably spelled out in Jawadarlal' Nehru's, <u>The Dis-</u>
<u>covery of India</u>, first published 1946.

39. See "The Third World Employment Crisis and the Multinationals. The ILO group confers, the Groupp of 77 agitates
-- what can the Multinationals do about it?", <u>Multinatio-</u>
<u>nal Business</u>, 1976, III, p.12.

40. Berg, A., "Industry's Struggle with World Malnutrition",
<u>Harvard Business Review</u>, January-February 1972, p.134.

REFERENCES

Bos, H.C., Sanders, M. and Secchi, C., <u>Private Foreign Invest-</u>
<u>ment in Developing Countries</u>, L; Reidel, 1974.

Cohen, Benjamin, <u>The Question of Imperialism</u>, Basic Books,
1973.

Helleiner, Gerald K., "Manufactures Exports from Less Developed Countries and Multinational Firms", <u>The Economic Jour-</u>
<u>nal</u>, March 1973.

Lall, Sanjaya and Streeten, Paul, <u>Foreign Investment, Trans-</u>
<u>nationals and Developing Countries</u>, MacMillan Press, 1977.

Meier, Gerald M., <u>Problems for Cooperation for Development</u>,
Oxford University Press, 1974.

Radice, Hugo (ed.), <u>International Firms and Modern Imperial-</u>
<u>ism</u>, Penguin Series, 1975.

Rosenstein Rodan, P.N., Multinational Investment in the Framework of Latin American Integration, Interamerican Bank, April 1969.

Streeten, Paul, "The Multinational Enterprise and the Theory of Development Policy", World Development, October 1973.

Streeten, Paul, "Costs and Benefits of Multinational Enterprises in Less Developed Countries", Dunning, J. (ed.), The Multinational Enterprise, Praeger, 1971.

Tharakan, P.K.M., Multinational Companies and a New International Division of Labour, (first version), European Centre for Study and Information on Multinational Corporations, Brussels, 1978

Vaitsos, Constantine, Intercountry Income Distribution and Transnational Enterprises, Clarendon Press, 1974.

Monographs on specific developing countries such as:
Kidron, Michael, Foreign Investment in India, 1965.
Newfarmer, R and Mueller, Willard F., Multinational Corporations in Brasil and Mexico. Structural Sources and Noneconomic Power, Washington, GPO, 1975.

4 LABOUR UNIONS AND THE NIEO PROGRAMME. SOME REMARKS ON THE POSITION OF LABOUR IN INDUSTRIALISED COUNTRIES

Kurt P. Tudyka

4.1. INTRODUCTION

If asked, everybody today would probably endorse general goals like worldwide social progress and justice, mutual understanding, equality of rights among nations and close cooperation between developing and industrialized countries - as these are envisaged by the U.N. 'International Economic Order' and by the 'Programme of Action on the Establishment of a New International Economic Order'. (1)

For several decades now, similar ideas have been expressed in quite a lot of the programs, declarations, resolutions, etc., of labour unions all over the world. (2) It can be left moot here whether or not labour unions in industrialized countries paid real earlier attention - or only lip service - to the problems of developing countries than did other groups. (3) The fact is, the U.N. program for a new international economic order proclaims to a certain extent much more than the labour unions, vague ideals on welfare and development. It essentially includes the proposal for a new internatiocal division of labour, which would necessarily have a far-reaching impact on the status quo of the workers in industrialized countries. One may well wonder whether labour unions in industrialized countries can, wholeheartedly and without any reservations, subscribe to such a strategy, which could directly reduce the employment and income of their members. (4)

The U.N. resolutions gave the International Confederation of Free Trade Unions (I.C.F.T.U.) cause to formulate a 'Development Charter'. (5) The ICFTU is the association of labour unions in the Western world with the largest amount of members. A solid majority of them are - like majorities of many other international nongovernmental organizations - from Western Europe, which determines finally the program and the policy of the Confederation. (6) It is therefore certainly not distorting to consider ICFTU statements as representative for most influential labour unions in the industrialized countries outside the U.S.A. (7)

During the last couple of years the labour unions have had, more than before, to elaborate their position on various real issues of the world economy and to respond practically to a changed economic and political environment - e.g. the spread, operations and profits of multinational corporations, the so-called energy crisis, world inflation, speculations on the commodity and money markets, the evaporation of jobs, the general economic recession. (8) With respect to all these problems labour unions had reasons enough to regard the present state of the international economy as very critical. Therefore, their conclusion that a new economic order would be in the interest of the peoples of developing and industrialized countries alike, is hardly surprising. In the tradition of an understanding that cannot isolate the economy from the total society, the labour unions consider furthermore the 'creation of a new social order' as 'essential' as the establishment of a new economic order; 'progress towards both must proceed in parallel' because existing international economic relations 'harm working people everywhere'. (9)
    In the following, we will describe and comment on the labour unions' criticism of the - in their own words - present 'chaotic and deteriorated international economic relations', their proposals for a new policy for the developing and industrialized countries, and finally the role and functions which the labour unions see for themselves with respect to the new international economic order.

4.2. THE DETERIORATED AND CHAOTIC WORLD ECONOMIC RELATIONS

The labour unions take for granted and as well-known 'that the "laissez-faire formula" of development through profits and competition has created growing and unacceptable inequalities'. (10) The orientation towards fast economic growth, rapid industrialization and exports under the assumptions of concepts like the 'trickle down' idea of economic growth has 'proved completely unrealistic mainly because of the rigidity of social and institutional structures and the dominant economic power of landlords and merchant-money lenders in developing societies'. (11) It seems that this structural criticism is rather limited regarding the situation of the so-called 'traditional sector', whose conditions are not seen as a result of the world economy, i.e. according to the unions, the pauperization of the southern hemisphere is not the result of the world economic system, but quite the contrary - the world economic system could and can not function because of the poverty in the developing countries. (12)
    On the other hand, however, the labour unions maintain bluntly that most of the 'failures' of the present system of international economic relations are an outcome of the 'normal', industrial, financial and commercial activities of <u>multinational corporations</u> which impose their private planning on economies to the detriment of public planning. The multinationals 'may in many cases virtually decide whether a

country is to expand its production and employment or, alter-
natively, to stagnate'. (13) Their operations 'may have an
inherent inflationary effect, quite apart from any price-
hiking possibilities arising from their position of market
domination'. (14) And the developing countries will not necessarily receive the industrial investment that is best
suited to their real development needs and they are not
certain how long the companies will continue production in
the country. (15) In the labour unions' opinion, the companies are thus responsible 'for perpetuating the world's economic imbalance and further widening the gap between rich
and poor nations'. (16)

These are some of the more purely economic complaints of labour unions against the multinational corporations. There
are two other important political complaints: these companies 'owe no allegiance to any nation state' and 'they mostly seek to escape any form of democratic control or social
responsibility'. (17)

In particular labour unions have denounced the 'undermining
of national independence by multinational corporations' because they take decisions 'thousands of miles away' - affecting the lives of people and 'to the detriment of democratic
decision-making by national governments'. (18)
    There is a whole catalogue of various issues which the
unions have brought forward again and again in attacking the
practices of the multinationals. (19) This criticism very
often ranges from charges to simple laments and consists of
a collection of facts, probabilities and possibilities. In
other words, the accusations have in general an unspecific
character.
    In this manner the labour unions assert, e.g., that the
multinational corporations can 'juggle exports and imports
by fixing artificial prices for transfers between the parent
firm and/or its foreign subsidiaries' and that they can
'manipulate dividends, tax payments and capital movements in
ways which often escape the control of national authorities'.
(20) In the labour unions' opinion such practices have had
'serious repercussions on the implementation of the policies
of many governments in respect of the balance of payments,
domestic industrial development, inflation and national economic planning' especially, by inference, as 'by some of
these companies' in the international political affairs of
countries: 'The methods used have ranged from the large-scale
bribery of politicians to the active promotion of subversive
movements aiming at the overthrow of democratically-elected
governments'. (21) Through all this, the companies had extracted far-reaching concessions, for instance, tax holidays
for up to ten years, exemption from import duties; they had,
further, made use of their freedom from the increasingly
stringent anti-pollution and health-protection measures being
adopted in the older industrialized countries. And 'most des-
picable of all', the companies had got guarantees against labour union 'interference' in the shape of 'restrictive legislation for ensuring the trouble-free exploitation of vast

pools of cheap labour'. (22) Finally in this context the labour unions denounce 'some' multinational corporations for
their alleged preference for investing in countries 'with dic-
tatorial regimes, where elementary human and labour rights are
systematically flouted'. (23)

The labour unions depreciate in general the value of the investments, the access to foreign currency from increased exports, etc., which the developing countries get in return for
the activities of multinational corporations on their soil.
They mention, however, as a 'side effect of the superprofit-
making activities' of the multinational corporations in developing countries, 'the stimulus they give to protectionist
feelings and the jeopardizing of support for development aid
policies among workers in industries affected by unfair competition in the older industrial countries'. (24) One may wonder whether the attitude of workers can so easily be explained. (25)

The second main political charge against multinational corporations has to do with the activities of the labour unions
themselves. It is obvious for them 'that the growth and concentration of international capital must tip the balance of
bargaining power in favour of management and against labour'.
(26) The reason for that is - a situation the labour unions
thus concede - 'the absence of coordinated international trade
union action'. (27) The possible consequences of this situation were, during the last decade, very often expounded and
widely publicised by the labour unions: 'Strikes can be broken
by the transfer of production to other factories of the same
company; the introduction of industrial democracy can be rendered null and void, if the board of directors on which the
workers are granted representation is autonomous but subject
to control from a parent body in another country', etc. (28)

Undoubtedly the labour unions focus their complaint of the
state of international economic relations on the operations
of multinational corporations - or, better, on the misuse
which is made or can be made of the concentration of economic
and political power. By doing so they try to alarm the national governments and the international organizations from which
they expect decisive measures - last but not least - in order
'to put an end to the frantic competition between nations to
secure investment and jobs from the multinationals'. (29)

It seems remarkable that both the unions' analysis and their
proposed programmes for action avoid almost any differentiation among national governments, not to speak of criticism of
them. It is amazing that they thereby draw such a sharp line
between the effects of business ('as usual') done by multinational corporations and the effects of policies carried out
by national governments. This stupendous picture of an (at
least latently) inherent contradiction between the interests
of multinational corporations and those of governments can
only be justified with the assumption that the governments
represent (or are legitimized by) the national population resp.

the forthcoming national bourgeoisie, while the multinational corporations stand for a power-hungry, corrupt sort of
international monopolistic finance capital. In such a view
there is no place for the supposition that the fate of quite
a lot of governments all over the world is interrelated with
that of multinational corporations. Thus the criticism of the
labour unions does not rest on the analysis of the 'international society', i.e. the social relations and the mode of
production, the social classes and the hegemonic powers, etc.,
but on an eclectic summary of failures and shortcomings of the
present system. What consequences such a superficial approach
has for the formulation of a programme of action we will see
in the following section - but one fundamental argument of the
labour unions is obvious: it is not the present international
system or its structure which is made responsible for the
existing problems, but a number of particular operations within this system.

4.3. TOWARDS ANOTHER GOVERNMENTAL POLICY

The labour unions speak through their 'Development Charter'
mainly to the national governments both in industrialized and
developing countries whose activities they try to stimulate.
In this regard one could summarize their ideas as follows:
The governments should
1. pursue economic policies seeking to create employment and
   to satisfy basic needs,
2. impose international surveillance on a number of transactions, and
3. make unions an element of a new national and international
   institutional framework for the realization of those policies which are devoted to the building of a new international economic and social order.

4.3.1. The governments as agents for more employment and de-
       velopment

The labour unions expect numerous decisions by governments
which would induce 'useful production everywhere'. They suppose apparently that governments in general have the power to
intervene in the economy and to bring about such effects. They
call for public support of local and regional organizations,
especially of course for initiatives coming from the unions
themselves. The common view of the labour unions - as it is
expressed in the 'developing charter' of the ICFTU - differ-
entiates governments according to the 'stage' of the development of their countries, i.e. the distinction is between the
required policy of a developing country and that of an industrialized country; but the labour unions do not distinguish
between countries with more or less 'mixed economies' and not
at all between the limits and possibilities of intervention
in a capitalist as against a socialist society.

4.3.1.1. The tasks of governments in developing countries
The labour unions call upon the developing countries to re-
assess their development objectives in favour of a 'basic
needs strategy' because 'the growth-orientated strategies of
the past, based on rapid industrialization and exports, have
brought little benefit to the mass of the people'. (30)
   The concept of 'basic needs' is undoubtedly a very ambi-
gious one. What do the unions have in mind, when in line with
the 1976 ILO World Employment Conference they require that
governments should follow an 'active reform policy', an economic policy adapted to a strategy of satisfying the basic
needs of the population, and that this strategy 'should become an essential part of any development programme and form
the core of the U.N. Third Development Decade'? (31)
Essentially they want 'family consumption' (food and clothing,
decent housing), vital community services (safe drinking water, proper sanitation, medical care, educational facilities,
public transport) and adequate jobs and union rights. (32)
   One must notice that the labour unions' basic needs concept is nothing more than the attempt to support a counter-
strategy to conventional economic growth policy. For all the
possible implications of this strategy they refer themselves
to information expected from subsequent ILO conferences and
from various studies in progress undertaken by different U.N.
organizations, e.g. the World Bank. (33) Nevertheless, they
already announce an <u>implementation</u> of basic needs strategies
as one of their main objectives – and they define their wage
policy as a part thereof. The labour unions maintain furthermore that the basic needs approach is not only of a 'progressive social nature' but also that it makes 'economic sense',
because raising the standard of living of the mass of the
people will boost consumption levels and thereby create the
international market which is necessary for self-sustaining
growth. (34)
   In the opinion of the labour unions – as it is expressed
in their 'development charter' – the proper role of industries
in developing countries should be mainly the production of
goods for the <u>domestic</u> markets. Therefore, the purchasing
power of the whole population should be 'considerably' increased, but the production should be geared 'to the basic
needs of the people'. (35)

4.3.1.2. The task of governments in industrialized countries
The labour unions acknowledge that structural changes with
negative consequences for employment will be also unavoidable
in the future of the industrialized countries. In order that
workers of the suffering industries do not bear the burden of
the necessary changes, the labour unions ask the governments
of the industrialized countries to take the initiative in a
series of policies. But they are not very outspoken with respect to the kind of 'countervailing measures to create alternative jobs' they mean. The situation in each of the industrialized countries where these unions operate seems to be too
unique to allow the formulation of a common long-term economic
policy for all unions. They agree that, in general, reflation-
ary measures should be the special duty of the key industrial-

ized countries and that emphasis should be placed on improving public services. (36)
 The export of industrial goods from developing countries
to the industrialized countries remains <u>the</u> crucial problem
for the labour unions in the industrialized countries. Certainly most of them endorse trade liberalization through the
multilateral trade negotions of the General Agreement on Tariffs and Trade. Furthermore, many labour unions - probably
a majority - support the granting of special preferences to
developing countries. (37)

But the labour unions are not unconditionally 'free traders'.
They may recognize trade liberalization as a necessary means
for developing countries to earn sufficient foreign exchange
to pursue their development strategy, i.e. to pay for essential imports - from industrialized countries! In this context
the unions even accept as well a preferential treatment of
products from developing countries as - self-limitation agreements. But even under these conditions they demand certain
very specific restrictions which are directly connected with
the labour market. They want to introduce numerous regulations
to avoid a ruinous competition among workers of various countries. In general they ask for the prohibition of imported
goods which are produced 'under conditions which endanger
workers' health and lives'. In particular they call for new
rules for international trade 'so as to ensure that exporters
in the developing countries meet minimum fair labour standards'... and 'respect ....minimum social standards'. (38)

4.3.2. The promises of the international governmental organi-
        zations

The labour unions are obviously very much aware of the fact
that international organizations like those of the U.N. system are institutions which depend in may regards - decision-
making, financing, personnel, policy implementation - upon the
willingness of national governments to cooperate. Consequently
they address the governments in the first line to use the instrument of the international organizations in order to facilitate development policy. They seem to believe that the establishment of a new international economic (and social) order
lies in the enlightened national interest of these governments.
On the other hand, the labour unions are rather modest in regard to demands for new covenants, codes or for the establishment of new international institutions. Instead of calls for
new initiatives they appeal to the national governments to
ratify and to apply extensively the already existing conventions, resolutions, recommendations, programmes for actions,
etc., of various international organizations like the ILO and
UNCTAD or of the many international conferences like the World
Population Conference, HABITAT, and especially the International Labour Conferences.

The labour unions expect from the GATT Multilateral Trade Negotiations not only a reduction of tariffs and non-tariff bar-

riers - this in line with the NIEO programme - but they also
demand the inclusion of a social clause (for the already-men-
tioned minimum wage and health standards) to the so-called
GATT-safeguard system. (39)

They seek to ensure that the existing voluntary agreements
on the code of conduct of multinational corporations - both
the Tripartite Declaration adopted by the ILO in 1977 and the
OECD Guidelines adopted in 1976 - are everywhere implemented.
They would of course prefer the introduction of binding international controls, a universal mandatory U.N. code equipped
with precise provisions for review and the imposition of sanc-
tions. (40)

It is only another aspect of the same problematic, namely
the transfer of technology 'on fair and equitable terms',
where the labour unions also insist upon international agreements through negotiations with UNCTAD; in particular they
want a mandatory code of conduct for the transfer of technology and a revision of the 1883 Paris Convention for the Protection of Industrial Property, 'which has strenghtened the
multinations' monopoly held over modern technology, and star-
ved developing countries of the technological know-how they
so badly need'. (41)

The labour unions want - in this context, with priority - the
implementation of a number of ILO conventions; they emphasize
especially convention 87 on freedom of association, convention 98 on collective bargaining, convention 131 on minimum
wages of unorganized workers and convention 141 on rural workers' organizations. (42)

Altogether they are more or less, and with the mentioned marginal notes, strongly in favour of the U.N. Declarations and
Programme of Action for the Establishment of a New International Economic Order. These documents express to a great extent the attitude and policy line of the mainstream of labour
unions in the industrialized countries. (43)

4.3.3. The participation of the labour unions

The labour unions not only wish to express their views with
respect to international social economic relations, they also
offer their active (political) participation in the process
of the implementation of the new international economic order.
Their programme contains a variety of proposals which aim at
fostering their position in the national and international
institutional network.

Their first goal, also in this context, is to broaden the
freedom of association. The labour unions claim that they already play a 'vital part in the fight for humane, democratic
and efficient societies', but that this role with respect to
development issues will never be effective without full freedom of association; i.e. freedom to unionize: 'working people
need it in the face of state power and the growing concentration of capital, whatever the nature of its ownership. Governments need it as an essential element in rational balanced and

efficient economic and social development'. (44)
    This is a very remarkable rationale; it rests upon two dif-
ferent and, to a certain degree, contradictory arguments:
unionizing is good for the interests of people facing bureau-
cratization and industrialization on a large scale; it is also good for effective policy implementation to have people organized. In other words, the labour unions emphasize their
possible function as legitimizing agencies of the ruling system. From this kind of pragmatic reasoning it is a far cry to
the traditional pathetic claim that the 'trade union movement'
bears a 'historic mission which would fail, if it was not concerned about fundamental social values, equally applicable in
developing and industrialized countries'. (45)
    The labour unions of the industrialized countries also par-
ticipate in various ways in an advisory function in the governmental process with respect to the shaping of the development policy. On the grounds of the ILO constitution, which
provides for a tripartite system (governments/employees/em-
ployers), they are official members of the national delegations to the conferences and to the council meetings. The international federations, e.g. the ICFTU, have consultative
status with many other organizations of the U.N. system; this
is often formally institutionalized, as e.g., with the OECD.
The labour unions want to strengthen (e.g., within the UNIDO
sectoral consultative system) and to extend their involvement.
    The ICFTU for instance, has urged that a consultative sys-
tem be set up by GATT 'whereby trade unions and employers'
organizations can discuss and reach agreements about long-term
changes in trade insofar as they affect employment and social
conditions'. (46)
The labour unions would like to be closely involved in the
work of the Committee on Industrial Cooperation and the Centre for Industrial Development established by the Lomé Convention. (47) They ask the government to agree upon permanent
tripartite consultative machinery within the United Nations
Environment Programme to evaluate the environmental impact of
industrial projects, etc. (48)
    In general, the labour unions come forward with the state-
ment: 'Each country should have a national commission dealing
with employment and basic needs. The commission should be
tripartite, with equal numbers of government, employers' and
workers' representatives, the latter being nominated by the
most representative trade union organization'. (49)
    Undoubtedly the labour unions think that they have a
'vital and executive role to play' not only with respect to the
narrow policy of development assistance but also in the broader context of the Third Development Decade.

4.4. LABOUR UNIONS WITHOUT STRATEGY AND ALTERNATIVES: CONCLUD-
     ING REMARKS

Nobody can expect that labour unions in industrialized countries would follow a 'strategy' which one could label to be
anti-capitalistic, socialistic or revolutionary, whatever
these terms would mean. Nevertheless they still claim to

participate in 'the fight of mankind for its full liberation. (50) The 'Development Charter' of ICFTU, however, is hardly a moderate reformistic program for the international social and economic relations of the future. (51)

Both the 'Development Charter' of the labour unions and the U.N. resolutions for a New International Economic Order - which are essentially in accordance - subscribe in fact to the present international structure of the social economic system, because none of the proposals aim to replace the system but rather to improve and to stabilize it. This can be proved in many ways; e.g., what do the labour unions require in order to deal with the problems of multinational corporations? In spite of all their (rhetorical) criticisms of those companies, the unions never demanded their dismantling or any form of socialization resp. nationalization. Consequently the labour unions agree with the OECD and the U.N. codes of conduct for the multinational corporations, which state that these companies are an important instrument for development.

The 'Development Charter' of the labour unions is comprised of 101 items; it is also very symptomatic for the orientation of the unions' policy that only three small items of the total of 101 deal with 'international labour solidarity'. These three paragraphs do not contain anything on class consciousness or on a common (objective) position of workers all over the world in the context of an extended international capitalist mode of production. Instead of such concepts, which were very familiar to the labour movement before World War II, these paragraphs deal with established rights in the U.N. system, with standards of health and safety and with education.

The labour unions in the industrialized countries are very much incorporated with the national state and the national (free market) economy of their respective countries. This is the result of the history of the working class over the last one hundred years: the once labour movement and its organizations, especially the labour unions, became more and more a stable and stabilizing element of the social and economic fabric of the bourgeois national state without any authentic strategies of their own or alternatives to the existing system.

FOOTNOTES

1. United Nations General Assembly resolutions 3201 (S-VI) and 3202 (S-VI)

2. See Ulrike Mertes: "Dokumentation gewerkschaftlicher Stellungnahmen zu entwicklungspolitischen Fragen", in Leminsky/Otto (ed.) Gewerkschaften und Entwicklungspolitik, Cologne 1975; World Confederation of Labour (ed.), The Development, Trade Union Positions and Proposals. World Trade Union Conference on Development. Geneva, 10-12 September 1973.

3. For information about the little or one-sided attention paid by British and U.S. labour unions to the problems of 'colonies' or 'backward countries', see Jeffrey Harrod, Trade Union Foreign Policy, New York 1972, p. 103-134.

4. This is one conclusion of a study done by Prognos AG, International Division of Labour: Present state and reform proposals. Commissioned by the International Metalworkers Federation, Basel 1977, p. 68.

5. 'Towards a New Economic and Social Order' - The ICFTU Development Charter, adopted by the 70th Meeting of the ICFTU Executive Board (Hamburg, 17-19 May 1978).

6. Of the about 50 million organized workers which through their national federations, are members of the ICFTU, more than 50 percent live in Western European countries; the most influenctial federations of unions are the British TUC and the West German DGB.

7. The U.S. federation AFL-CIO withdrew from the ICFTU because of its policy towards labour unions in Eastern Europe.

8. See the reports of the Conference on the World Economy of the ICFTU, Geneva, 24-26 June 1971, Brussels.

9. 'Towards a New ... ', p. 1.

10. Ibid., p. 15.

11. Ibid., p. 16.

12. The authors of the 'charter' are not outspoken on the causes of underdevelopment; on one hand, they blame laissez-faire formulas, on the other they ignore alternative approaches, e.g. the concept of self-reliance.

13. Multinational Charter, XI. World Congress documents, ed. by International Confederation of Free Trade Unions, Brussels 1975, p. 21.

14. Ibid., p. 21.

15. Ibid., p. 22.

16. Ibid., p. 21.

17. Ibid., p. 22.

18. Ibid., p. 22.

19. See, e.g., The Multinational Challenge, ICFTU World Economic Conference Reports no. 2, ed. by the ICFTU, Brussels 1971.

20. Multinational Charter ..., p. 22.

21. Ibid., p. 22.

22. Ibid., p. 22.

23. Ibid., p. 23.

24. Ibid., p. 22.

25. See for the complexity of this question: Attitudes and objectives of industrial manual workers on development issues. A Pilot Survey in France, the Federal Republic of Germany and Sweden, ed. by Ruth Padrun, IRFED/Action for Development, FAO Rome, 1972.

26. Multinational Charter, p. 23.

27. Ibid., p. 23.

28. Ibid., p. 23.

29. Ibid., p. 23.

30. 'Towards a New ...', p. 4.

31. Ibid., p. 4.

32. Ibid., p. 1, p. 15.

33. Ibid., p. 15.

34. Ibid., p. 4.

35. Ibid., p. 3.

36. Ibid., p. 2.

37. Ibid., p. 2.

38. Ibid., p. 3.

39. Articles 19 and 20 of GATT.

40. 'Towards a New ...', p. 3.

41. Ibid., p. 13.

42. Ibid., p. 6, pp. 23-24.

43. There are of course, within as well as without the ICFTU, more protectionistic, less programmatic and outspoken business-oriented unions, as there are more progressive and even socialistic-minded organizations; see, e.g., Jack Barbash, Trade Unions and National Economic Policy, Baltimore/London 1972.

44. 'Towards a New ...', p. 6.

45. Ibid., p. 1.

46. Ibid., p. 3.

47. Ibid., p. 8.

48. Ibid., p. 11.

49. Ibid., p. 16.

50. Ibid., p. 6.

51. See e.g. the evaluation of the World Council of Churches Central Committee: Statement on the New International Economic Order, Document No. 330, Geneva, July 28 - August 6, 1977.

REFERENCES

Böll, Winfried, "Gewerkschaften und Dritte Welt", in: Gewerkschaftliche Politik. Reform aus Solidarität, edited by Ulrich Bosdorf a.o., Bund Verlag, Köln, 1977.

Hero, Alfred O., Starr, Emil, The Reuther-Meany Foreign Policy Dispute. Union Leaders and Members View World Affairs, Oceana Publ., New York, 1970.

Jeuken, Piet, De Derde Wereld en Vakbondsleden in Nederland, in: Labour, Vol. 55, No. 2, February 1977.

Jeuken, Piet, "The Dutch Trade Union Movement and Assistance to the Unions of the Third World", in: Free Labour World, June 1975.

Leminsky, Gerhard, Otto Bernd (ed.), Gewerkschaften und Entwicklungspolitik, Bund Verlag, Köln, 1975.

Nelissen, Bert, De Internationale Vakbewegingen en Latijns Amerika, Utrecht, 1974.

Padrun, Ruth (ed.), Attitudes and Objectives of Industrial Manual Workers on Development Issues. A Pilot Survey in France, the Federal Republic of Germany and Sweden, IRFED/Action for Development, FAO, Rome, 1972 (mimeo).

Radosh, Ronald, American Labour and United States Foreign Policy, Random House, New York, 1969.

Wedin, Ake, International Trade Union Solidarity, ICFTU 1975-1965, Stockholm, 1974.

World Conference of Labour (ed.), The Development Trade Union Positions and Proposals, World Trade Union Conference on Development, Geneva, 10-23 September 1973.

5 INTERNATIONAL INDUSTRIAL RELOCATION. SOME FACTORS OF CHANGE

Ben H. Evers

5.1. INTRODUCTION

The position and the role in the world economic system of
part of the developing world is expected to change significantly in the future. Increasing industrial exports are becoming a realistic perspective for many developing countries.
The first clear signals for such a change could already be
observed at the end of the 1960's and in the early 1970's. In
the period 1962-1970 developing countries managed to retain a
more or less stable market share in the imports of the twenty-
one main industrialized countries. In view of the rapidly expanding mutual relations between the latter group of countries, this was not a minor achievement.

In the period 1970-1976 imports of manufactures (1) by industrialized countries from developing countries accelerated
to an unprecedented average of 26 percent annually. This was
translated into an increase in the market share of developing
countries from 4.9 percent in 1970 to 6.3 percent in 1975 and
7.3 percent in 1976. (2) Initially, this trade was mainly restricted to relatively few product categories (such as clothing, textiles, leather and footwear, components for the
electrotechnical industry, etc.) and concentrated on a limited number of developing countries (such as Hong Kong, Singa-
pore, Taiwan, S.Korea, Brazil, Mexico).

For the future, however, one can foresee that more developing countries will succeed in penetrating the markets of the
industrialized countries with a much wider range of industrial products. Both push and pull variables will be instru-

---

*) This chapter is based on report No.10 of the research
group on industrial readjustment and the international division of labour. See: B.Evers, G.de Groot, W.Wagenmans:
Perspectives on Industrial Readjustment; the EEC and the
Developing Countries, Tilburg, 1978 . (see also Annex I)

mental in this regard -- push variables to be understood as
the pressures on industrialized countries towards increased
internationalization of production, pull variables as the
pressures on developing countries towards increased export-
oriented industrialization.

In this paper some preliminary ideas are formulated regarding future developments in the international location of industrial activities. Because the growth, the structure, the
geographical pattern and the distribution of costs and benefits of these exports are strongly influenced by developments
in the industrialized countries in view of their dominant position in international economic relations, the emphasis in
this chapter will be placed on the latter category of countries, paying special attention to the EEC.

We start by briefly indicating some of the major characteristics of the process of international economic development
during the past three decades. Increasing internationalization of production and trade (in particular between the industrialized countries) combined with rapid technological innovation and diffusion are some of the crucial factors in explaining the dynamism of the industrialized countries. However, in the early 1970's it became apparent that this model
was beginning to show signs of exhaustion and that profound
readjustments, both on a national and international scale,
are needed to introduce a new dynamism. This readjustment
process will have important repercussions on the role of the
developing countries.

Next, we sketch a "scenario" of a possible structure of
future economic growth of the EEC within the international
context. This may serve as a frame of reference for analyzing
the transfer process of productive activities to low-wage
countries in which European industry is involved.

The tendency towards relocation will not be equally strong
for all kinds of industrial activities. The body of this
chapter consists of a more detailed analysis of the pressure
on different kinds of industrial activities to be transferred
to developing countries.

5.2. FROM MONO- TO MULTIPOLARITY IN INTERNATIONAL ECONOMIC
     RELATIONS

The international economic development of the past three decades can be characterized by the following elements:
- an accelerated growth of industrial production in both developed and developing countries (period 1950/52 to 1967/69;
  annual compound growth rates of industrial production: USA
  4.0 percent, Europe 7.1 percent, other developed countries
  7.9 percent, developing countries 6.8 percent, world average 5.9 percent; (3)
- an increasing degree of homogeneity in the structures of
  production and consumption in the more developed industrial
  countries;
- a change in the economic prominence of the different indus-

trial countries, revealing a tendency to move from mono- to multipolarity in international economic relations (percentage share in world industrial production in 1950 resp. 1969: USA 45 resp. 33 percent, Europe 39 resp. 48 percent, other developed countries 7 resp. 9 percent, developing countries 9 resp. 10 percent); (4)

- an intensification of the international division of labour and a higher degree of interdependence between the economies of the industrial countries, mainly based on intrasectoral specialization;
- an acceleration of the process of centralization and concentration of capital, leading to an increasing superiority of a limited number of large companies on the national economic level as well as in the field of international investment and trade. This trend can be observed in the areas of industrial production, of finance and of trade (for example, intrafirm trade within MNE's is already estimated at 45 percent of total world trade; (5)
- an increasing participation of Western capital in the industrialization process of developing countries;
- the emergence of enclave-like export industries in a number of developing countries almost entirely dominated by Western industrial and/or commercial firms. The utilization of cheap local labour forms almost the only link with the national economy;
- an increasing dependency of industrial countries on raw materials imports from developing countries.

The economic problems of the 1970's have revealed a large measure of instability in the Western economic system, specifically in the areas of growth, trade, investments, monetary relations. etc.. The recession has made apparent that in the past a great deal of industrial adjustment took place without causing serious problems (with the exception of regional imbalances). On the other hand it has demonstrated that further readjustment is unavoidable. However, frictions created by adjustments in a period of slow economic expansion are much harder to tackle.

Some of the adjustment problems emanate from the increased competition of industrial products from developing countries. However, it would be incorrect to consider the change in the structure of trade between developed and developing countries as the result of a more or less successful industrialization policy on the part of the developing countries. On the contrary, it is basically the outcome of a shift in emphasis in the internationalization process of Western capital.

On the one hand MNE's clearly display a tendency to increase the transfer of specifically their labour-intensive production activities to so-called low-wage countries. On the other hand, this is also closely bound up with a change in the structure of commerce.

The concentration of commercial capital has enabled a number of trading houses (both wholesale and retail trade) to develop a global scanning capacity. This means they have developed the capacity to utilize on an international scale the cheapest supply potentials of especially labour-intensive consumer goods, and - if necessary - to organize this supply themselves. In addition to having ample marketing experience, they have the means to organize local production in low-wage countries for export purposes and without necessarily using their own capital for productive investments. The resulting imports of industrial goods into developed countries are competitive to such a degree as to leave manufacturers no alternative but to proceed to transfer part of their productive activities to low-wage countries as well.

In this sense it would be incorrect to say that imports from developing countries are the real cause of adjustment problems in industrialized countries, notwithstanding claims to the contrary by some of the most affected social groups. The origin lies in the structure of the expansion of the capitalist system of the industrialized countries, in particular in the process of internationalization.

5.3. THE STRUCTURE OF FUTURE GROWTH AND TRADE: ELEMENTS OF A "SCENARIO"

Inasfar as the process of relocation of productive activities from developed to developing countries is strongly influenced by developments originating in the industrialized countries, it is necessary to indicate at least some of the major elements related to these developments. However, the ideas formulated here are very preliminary indeed. They are based upon a limited number of qualitative assessment elements, and not on a profound analysis.

With these limitations in mind, we think the following trends the most relevant ones:
- industrialized countries will be faced by a considerably lower average economic growth than in the past, one of the main reasons being the absence of new dynamic industries capable of magnetizing the rest of the economy. The breakthrough of potentially very dynamic industries will still encounter serious barriers either of a technological, a financial or a political nature. On the other hand, the consumer demand for certain categories of goods is showing signs of saturation. Thus, prospects at the medium term are characterized rather by a further expansion of existing industrial structures than by a drastic and rapid change of these structures;
- in view of the growing homogeneity of production and consumption structures of the industrialized countries, the less spectacular technological progress and the diminished growth, it can be anticipated that mutual trade between developed countries will be less dynamic than in the past. A somewhat more protectionist attitude can be expected, expressed particularly at a sectoral level and in the form of non-tariff barriers. Direct investments will continue to be instrumental to the penetration of each other's markets, in the course of which the investment stream from Europe and Japan to the USA will increase in significance. On the

other hand, trade in manufactures with developing countries is expected to accelerate;
- in the next ten to fifteen years unemployment might become a structural feature of industrialized countries as well (already now, unemployment is considerably higher than official statistics indicate). Economic growth will be relatively slow, technological development will remain of a labour-saving nature. Industry is already expected to diminish its demand for labour. A continuation of the trend to expand labour-intensive productive activities in low-wage countries is to be anticipated, a trend that will be hard to curb in view of the sharpened competition between industrial countries.
The services sector will be incapable of absorbing the available labour adequately; the private sector is expected to increasingly introduce labour-saving methods, the non-private sector is not expected to maintain its rate of expansion of the past in view of governmental budget limitations;
- limited wage rises, coupled with a drop in the growth rate of transfer allowances distributed through the public budget appear to justify the assumption that in future private consumption will show only a modest expansion in industrialized countries;
- to improve growth prospects for the EEC, emphasis will be placed on the expansion of the technology-intensive capital goods industry and on the promotion of exports, in particular to developing countries;
- as far as economic relations between industrialized and developing countries are concerned, several tendencies are apparent.

The tendency of the three centre areas to create and reaffirm their economic-geographical spheres of influence is on the increase. Japan is pursuing a consistent and dynamic policy vis-à-vis Southeast Asia, the EEC directs its efforts particularly to Africa and the Mediterranean, while the USA traditionally claims Latin America as its backyard. This applies to trade treaties, investment streams, etc., and to a similar extent to political and military alliances. However, this tendency is subject to considerable restrictions in view of the mounting mutual competition between the industrial countries. As a matter of fact, none of the three centres can economically afford to concentrate exclusively on these areas in case this would prove to be detrimental to their own competitive position. In this context, the differences in degree and kind of raw material dependency springs to mind, but also the variations in wage-costs, in particular in as far as these are codetermined by the possibility to import cheap industrial end-products and intermediate products from developing countries. In other words, even disregarding international power politics (also from the Socialist countries) a kind of vertical division of the world cannot be envisaged, in spite of tendencies towards regionalism.
At any rate, the developing world will, to our view con-

stitute the arena par excellence in which the growing compe-
tiveness of the centra will be exposed. On the other hand,
the necessity for industrialized countries to safeguard the
raw-materials supply might provide a number of producer countries the leverage for following a more independent industrialization strategy. Differences between the various developing countries in terms of economic structures and levels
of living might, however, become more pronounced.

5.4. PERSPECTIVES ON INDUSTRIAL RELOCATION

The major argument for the assumption that the tendency towards a relocation of productive activities to developing
countries will persist in the future is that present and ex-
pexted competetive relations among the industrialized countries -- or, rather, among the various internationally competing capital groups -- will enforce an intensification of the
search for the least expensive possibilities for supply on a
global scale. Slowing down this relocation of productive activities to countries with a low-wage level would lead to a
disadvantage in the competetive position of various capital
groups, which would be particularly detrimental to industries
which export an important part of their production (but not
only for these).
    Technical, financial and organizational capacities in cor-
porate business -- especially, but not exclusively, in MNE's
-- have been sufficiently developed to permit the actual realization of a further international diffusion of productive
activities. This tendency is reinforced by the developing
countries themselves, which offer very generous incentives
for the establishment of foreign export-oriented industries.
In addition, the developing countries are highly interested
in an increase in local industrial processing of their exported raw materials, and - more generally - in a higher participation in the world trade in industrial products. One could
thus speak of a push and pull effect.
    The tendency towards relocation will not be equally strong
for all industrial activities. In this section we will try to
present a first, albeit not detailed classification. As an
angle of view we choose the nature of the production process,
and we will also pay attention to competetive relations -- as
far as this is possible on this level.
    The nature of the production process allows a classifica-
tion of industries into four categories: processing industry,
semi-finals industry, specialized capital-goods industry and
assembling industry (see Figure 1).

It must be observed explicitly that this classification may
not necessarily apply to single corporations; on the contrary, it will often run transverse the structures of corporations. In our opinion, a classification such as this fits
the reality of the relocation process better than an approach
based on a branch - or individual firm - analysis. One can
observe that in many cases there is no relocation of corpora-

FIGURE 1

Position of types of industry in the production process

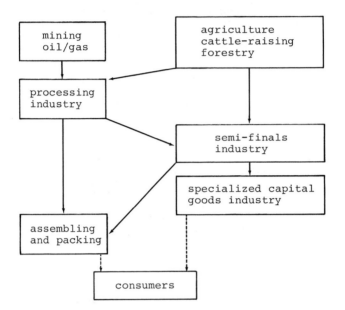

Source: Dr. Ir. K.Westerterp: "De toekomst van de procesin-
dustrie in Nederland", Inaugural address, Twente, May 1977.

tions, but rather of certain parts of the production processes of corporations. The same is true regarding the transfer
of branches of industry.

Of particular relevance with respect to competitive relations is the measure to which productive activities have been
internationalized, as well as the role played in this process
respectively by productive or commercial capital.

5.4.1. Processing industry

In the processing industry raw materials are transformed --
by way of a process -- into totally different products that
serve as input products for other industries. Therefore these
industries are found mainly in the first phases of raw material processing (extraction of metals from ore, chemical processes, generation of electricity, beer-brewing, coffee-roas-
ting, sugar-manufacturing, etc.).

A distinction can be made between processing industries
that use extractive resources and those that use agricultural

or animal products for raw materials. In the former, economies of scale play a very important part. They generally are
capital- and technology-intensive, and only slightly labour-
intensive.

In order to utilize the advantages of producing on a large
scale - under pressure of competition - a permanent high level of investment is necessary, which necessity is further
reinforced by technological development. As a result, industry is confronted regularly with problems of over-capacity.
Periods of intensive competition alternate with periods of
cartel-like cooperative connections. A continuous centralization process takes place. Production and distribution of especially the heavier processing industry are dominated by
multinational production corporations, and commercial capital
hardly plays an independent role.
    From the above it follows that differences in wage-levels
between countries are not an important factor in deciding the
locational pattern. On the ground of relative factor intensity one would expect this capital- and technology-intensive
industry to be preeminently suited for developed countries,
the more so as the availability of a large home market may be
an important basis.
    In spite of this, we believe on the ground of various ar-
guments that in the future there will be, to a certain extent, a relocation towards developing countries.
    In the first place we must consider that the strategy of a
growing number of developing countries is aimed at accelerating the industrialization process. In a number of countries
that have advanced further in establishing import-substituting industries, an important internal market has begun to
develop which offers ever more possibilities for parts of the
processing industry. The effect of this on European processing industry cannot yet be calculated. For where continuing
import substitution will reduce export possibilities, a beginning industrialization in other developing countries may
expand these possibilities again.
    In the second place - and more directly related to the re-
location issue - there is a growing pressure from raw-mate-
rials-producing countries to have their exports processed locally. Especially when the possibilities of these countries
to form cartels or use other means of power grow, the possibilities for establishing export-oriented processing industries in certain developing countries will increase. In view
of the growing scarcity of raw materials, the industrialized
countries might be faced with a structural raise in relative
prices. This will afford the producing countries greater possibilities for setting up processing industries which will be
to a large extent export-oriented. Already we can observe
that a number of developing countries are engaged in the accelerated setting up of industries in the fields of petroche-
mistry, fertilizers, man-made fibres, iron and steel, etc..
This industrialization takes place in cooperation with Western MNE's, as these still hold an enormous lead in technology and distribution.

We do not expect a very rapid relocation in the sense of a direct termination of productive activities in the West in order to stimulate their expansion in developing countries. The relocation process will be confined to the margine, i.e. the establishing of new investment projects will be increasingly located in developing countries. The implications of this for production in Europe are represented graphically in Figure 2.

FIGURE 2

Expected production volume of European processing industry

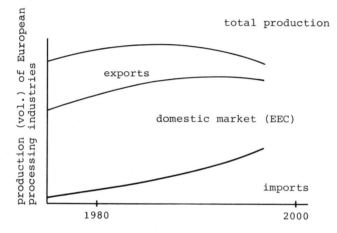

The fact that the slow-down of industrial growth in Europe will increase existing capacity problems and thus make it necessary to discard the least remunerative production units has been taken into account in the figure. Internationally, this will improve the competitive position of Europe somewhat. There will also be a pressure towards solving the capacity problems through exports and interfering with competing imports by way of market-protecting forms of cooperation. In connection with this we expect that the anti-cartel policy of the EEC will not be too intensive, as a number of these products might be characterized as being of strategic significance for the European economies. Policy will indeed be aimed at not becoming too dependent on imports for the provision of these products.

In other words, there are also factors that will hinder a very fast relocation, and, insofar as this relocation occurs, there will be an attempt to direct it to territories which are within the direct economic and political sphere of influence of Europe. In processing industries we often deal

with large investment projects -- in view of the importance
of the economies of scale. This constitutes an additional argument to be selective in relocation because of the great
economic and political risks.

In recapitulation, one can assume that the effects of relocation in terms of production and trade will emerge only
little by little in the next ten to fifteen years, and will
manifest themselves after that time in a more exponential
way.

The situation in the light processing industries (such as
food-processing, paint industry, filling-plants, etc.) cannot
be fully compared with this. Not only do economies of scale
play a less decisive role and is the technology element less
important, but a major difference is also that merchant capital forms a more independent factor. This type of processing
industry fits into the process of import-substituting industrialization in developing countries, while for parts possibilities also exist for exports to the markets of industrialized countries. In the latter, especially-developed countries' merchant capital will be actively involved, for example in the field of food processing.

The developments for heavy and light processing industries
sketched above have consequences for the structure of the
processing industries in Europe. The heavy industry will more
and more take to products and processes of a higher complexity of both the technology involved and the labour required
and will further specialize in much more efficient use of raw
materials. The rising prices of materials and energy, together with higher environmental demands, will necessitate new
material- and energy-saving technological developments (a
higher degree of chemical integration, substitution of certain raw materials, recycling materials, etc.; among process
improvements we may mention electro-chemistry, combustion
technology, membrane technology, biotechnology, powder technology, catalysis, etc.).

For lighter processing industry we expect a development
towards the production of goods with a lower price and a
higher income elasticity, for which aggressive marketing will
be important.

5.4.2. Semi-finals industry

The semi-finals industry processes elementary industrial outputs into intermediate products that serve as input for other
industries. Examples are fabrics, leather, fur, plywood, synthetic products, etc.. This type of industry covers a vast
area, which makes it difficult to present other than general
statements about the tendency of relocation towards developing countries. As for relative factor intensity it occupies
an intermediate position. It is neither markedly labour-intensive (like the assembling industry), nor capital-intensive
(like the processing industry), nor technology-intensive
(like the specialized capital goods industry).

For two reasons we expect a relocation of part of this industry to developing countries in the future. In the first
place, it concerns activities which rather quickly quality
for local production in countries which follow a strategy of
import-substituting industrialization. This will especially
have an impact on the export possibilities of Europe. In the
second place we expect a relocation of those parts of the
semi-finals industry that - while not highly concentrated
themselves - are clenched in between monopolistic input and
output industries. This category will not be able to pass on
raises in costs to their clients originating either in the
input side or in the manufacturing process. As far as the
advantages of the low costs of labour in developing countries
compensate the disadvantages of relocation, part of the semi-
finals industry will begin producing in developing countries
for markets in the industrialized countries.
  Since, in the full range of the semi-finals industry, the
substitution effect is probably more important quantitatively
than the relocation effect, we expect a gradual but limited
shift in the structure of production and trade for the next
ten to fifteen years.

5.4.3. Specialized capital-goods industry

In the specialized capital-goods industries machines are produced to measure or in small series for other industries and
corporations. Capital-goods industry concerns especially the
production of investment goods such as apparatuses for the
processing industry, packing and assembly machines, other
specialized machinery, etc.. This industry is not so much labour-intensive as capital- and research-intensive although
specific parts of this industry may be also labour-intensive
(e.g. construction). The branches in which these industries
operate are often structured hierarchically. They are dominated by a number of large corporations which in their production make an intensive use of a great number of small- to
medium-large suppliers. The latter also perform a buffer
function to absorb the trade cycles, which are rather strong
for these industries. Merchant capital hardly plays an independent role.
  The contribution of the developing countries to the world
production of capital goods has been marginal up to now. For
the future we expect a limited increase of their relative
contribution, especially on the ground of the prospects with
regard to the industrialization process in developing countries, an increase which will be realized through import substitution, particularly in those countries that dispose of a
large internal market and have already made progress in the
industrialization process (e.g. textile machines). Fundamental changes in the international structure of production and
trade in this type of goods by this limited increase are not
expected to occur, due to the enormous technological lead of
Western industry. Important exports from developing to industrialized countries in this field are therefore not foresee-

able in the near future.

In our opinion, the most important shifts will occur within Europe itself. The less favourable growth prospects, together with the need for high expenses on research and development will necessitate a process of increasing concentration. The pressure for this is raised by the existing capacity problems. Intensifying cooperation between corporations in this industry is facilitated by the fact that there is hardly any independent merchant capital; cooperation is hindered, however, by the occurrence of national contradictions within the EEC (e.g. ship-building). These contradictions are accentuated by the circumstance that most national administrations of the EEC have given priority to research-intensive industries in their industrial policies. As a consequence, the problems within this industry will have to be solved on a supra-national level.

5.4.4. Assembling industry

This industry uses intermediate products and components for the production of finished articles, which are transmitted through various trade channels to individual consumers. This mostly concerns consumer goods (like automobiles, television sets, radios, refrigerators, soft drinks, ready-made clothing, etc.), although the production of certain capital goods (e.g. trucks, simple standardized machines, etc.) may also be put in this category. The industry often is very labour-intensive, relatively seldom capital-intensive and seldom to moderately research-intensive.

Among the assembling industries we find branches which are little concentrated, but in which merchant capital plays an important role (e.g. clothing, foot-wear, furniture) along with branches which are dominated by multinational production corporations (e.g. electronics, automobiles). The first category is characterized by a very hich degree of labour intensity, using preferably low-skilled labour. Technological development is rather slow and so is the increase in labour productivity. Economies of scale are of limited significance as far as productive activities are concerned. Entry into the sector is relatively easy. The number of firms is large and many are family-owned. Management is often rather poor. Wage levels are below average industrial wages, making it difficult to obtain an adequate and sufficient labour supply.

In addition, these industries are confronted with an increasing degree of monopolization on the output side. The retail trade has gone through a process of concentration and integration, and purchases from these industries are made by an ever-decreasing number of decision centres. As consumption patterns became more homogenized, retail trade organizations were able to introduce a systematic policy of merchandizing. Once their needs were defined, price became the essential criterion in selecting suppliers on an international scale. Through direct investments (including joint ventures) or through commercial subcontracting (including sometimes tech-

nical assistance contracts) an important shift in the pattern
of international trade in this kind of product was originated.
International competition becoming stronger, the surviving
industries had no alternative but to internationalize their
production also, either by subcontracting work to firms
abroad or by transferring parts of their productive activities to low-wage countries by means of direct investment.

It is particularly in this type of assembling industries that
a major shift in the international division of labour between
industrialized and developing countries has occurred, and it
can be expected that this shift will persist in the future,
in particular for those kinds of products that are not very
susceptible to fashion or delivery time. In other words, in
our opinion the developing countries have a reasonable chance
to set up export production with local capital. It must be
observed, however, that these industries are very unstable
due to the high degree of dependence on both the internationally-operating merchant capital, and the trade policies of
importing industrialized countries.

Under present conditions, the establishment of this kind of
industrial activities in developing countries can hardly be
considered as a genuine contribution to development. For assembling industries that are dominated by multinational production corporations the relocation process is well under
way. The instability is somewhat less intense than for industries dominated by merchant capital because the MNE's set up
and spread production more systematically. Pursuing a European policy aimed at slowing down relocation of this type of
industry is very hard, if not impossible, in view of the international character and the power of the MNE's.

Some of above considerations are summarized as in Table 1.

Table 1

Perspectives of relocation of industries to developing countries

industries	factor intensities				relo-cation expec-tance
	labour	capital	tech-nical	natural resources	
Assembling	+	−	−/o	o	+
Semi-finals	o	o	o	o	o
Specialized capital goods	o	o/+	+	−	−
Processing	−	+	+	+	+

+   high
o   intermediate
−   low

5.5. CONCLUDING REMARKS

This has been no more than a tentative first consideration of possible changes in the structure of international production and trade in industrial products. The main agents of change are multinational production firms, internationally-operating trading firms, and governments in both industrial and developing countries. The direction of change is determined by such factors as technological development, competitive relations, policies of governments, etc.. It is only through a more detailed analysis of these agents and factors that firmer conclusions on future international relocation tendencies can be drawn.

In Figures 3 and 4 the major elements of such an analysis are presented graphically, Figure 3 applying to an assembling industry, Figure 4 to a processing industry.

FIGURE 3

The relocation process of the clothing industry

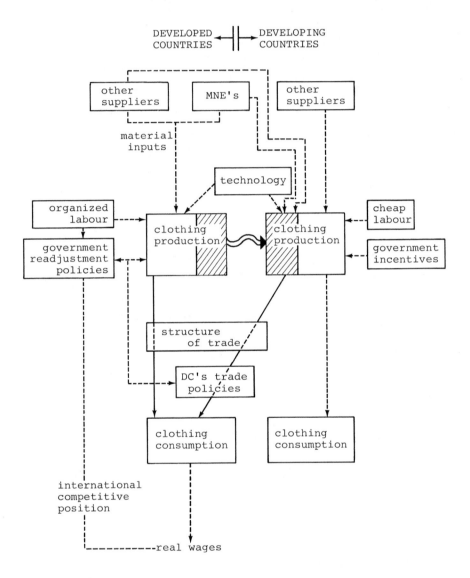

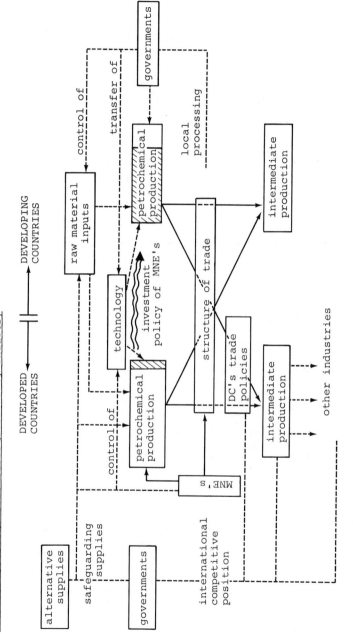

FIGURE 4

The relocation process of a processing industry

FOOTNOTES

1. Not including petroleum products and unwrought nonferrous metals.

2. Source of data: UNCTAD: TD/BC2/190.

3. U.N.: Economic Survey of Europe in 1971, Part I: The Economy from the 1950's to the 1970's, New York, 1972, p.3.

4. Idem.

5. Michalet, C.A.: Les Firmes Multinationals et la Nouvelle Division Internationale du Travail, ILO, Genève, 1975, p.32.

REFERENCES

Adam, G.: "Some implications and concomitants of worldwide sourcing", Acta Oeconomica, Vol. 8 (2-3), 1972, p.309-323.

Adjustment for Trade Studies on Industrial Adjustment Problems and Policies, OECD, 1975.

Becker-Boost, E.: "Industrialization in Developing Countries. Evaluation of Recent Progress and Appraisal of Prospects", in ed. Giersch, H.: Reshaping the World Economic Order, Kiel, Symposium 1976, p. 1-58.

Dicke, H., Glismann, H., Horn, E.J., Neu, A.: Beschäftigungswirkungen einer verstärkten Arbeitsteilung zwischen der Bundesrepublik und den Entwicklungsländern, Kieler Studien no. 137, 1976.

La Division Internationale du Travail:
    Volume I : Les tendences actuelles,
    Volume II: Trois scenarios prospectifs.
    Collection "Etudes de politique industrielle", Publiée par le Ministère de l'Industrie et de la Récherche à la Documentation Française, Parijs 1976.

Fröbel, F., Heinrichs, J., Kreye, O.: Die neue internationale Arbeitsteilung. Strukturelle Arbeitslosigkeit in den Industrieländern und die Industrialisierung der Entwicklungsländer, Reinbek bei Hamburg, 1977.

Groot, G. de: "Internationale Herstructurering, Staat en Vakbeweging", Paradogma, Vol. VIII, no. 2, September 1977, p. 11-44.

Helleiner, G.: "Manufactured Exports from Less-Developed Countries and Multinational Firms, The Economic Journal, Vol.83, March, 1973, p. 21-47.

Herman, B.: The Optimal International Division of Labour,
ILO, 1975.

Koekkoek, K., Kol, J., Mennes, L.: "De Nederlandse Industrie:
Concurrentievermogen, Comparatieve Voordelen en Goederen-
samenstelling van de Internationale Handel",
(I)   E.S.B., no. 3163, 19 July 1978, p. 720-723,
(II) E.S.B., no. 3164, 26 July 1978, p. 744-746,
(III) E.S.B., no. 3165, 2 August 1978, p. 768-772.

Mukherjee, S.: Free trade is good, but what about the workers? Trade liberalization and adjustment assistance,
P.E.P., London, March 1974.

Olle, W., Schoeller, W.: "Buitenlandse Produktie en Struktu-
rele Werkloosheid", Paradogma, Vol.IX, no.2, June 1978.

Research Project Industrial Readjustment and the Internatio-
nal Division of Labour, Development Research Institute,
Tilburg:
Report no. 1, Industrial Adjustment in the Netherlands,
with Special Reference to the Clothing Industry, May 1975.
Report no. 3, Industriële Herstructurering in Ontwikkelde
Landen en Industrialisatie in Ontwikkelingslanden, Septem-
ber 1975.
Report no. 7, Vlisco: Beoordeling van een Herstructure-
ringssubsidie, June 1977.
Report no. 8, Een Toekomst voor de Nederlandse Confectie-
Onderneming, June 1977.
Report no.10, Perspectives on Industrial Readjustment. The
EEC and the Developing Countries, February 1978.

De Structuur van de Nederlandse Economie en de Internationale
Arbeidsverdeling, Nationale Raad van Advies inzake Hulpver-
lening aan Minder Ontwikkelde Landen, Advies 31, 22 February 1971.

ANNEX I

- Industrial Adjustment in the Netherlands, with Special Reference to the Clothing Industry, Report No. 1, May 1975,
  43 pp., original Dutch;

- The Dutch Clothing Industry; Re-adjustment and the Development Dimension, Report No. 2, October 1975, 23 pp., original Dutch;

- Industrial Re-adjustment in Developed Countries and Industrialization of Developing Countries, Report No. 3, October
  1975, 18 pp., original Dutch;

- The European Clothing Industry; Problems and Developments,
  Report No. 4, December 1975, 47 pp., original Dutch;

- Tunesia; Perspectives of an Export-Oriented Industrialization, Report No. 5, March 1976, 60 pp., original Dutch;

- Hong-Kong; Development and Perspective of a Clothing Colony, Report No. 6, March 1977, 105 pp., original Dutch;
- Vlisco, Evaluation of a Re-adjustment Subsidy, Report No. 7, June 1977, 96 pp., original Dutch;
- A Future for the Dutch Clothing Industry, Report No. 8, June 1977, 157 pp., original Dutch;
- Repair or Renew; What is New in the New International Division of Labour, December 1977, 17 pp., original Dutch;
- Jobs and Values; Social Effects of Export-Oriented Industrialization in Tunesia, Report No. 9, December 1977, 78 pp., original English;
- Perspectives on Industrial Re-adjustment: The EEC and the Developing Countries, Report No. 10, February 1978, 98 pp., original English;
- Export Industry in Tunesia, Effects of a Dependent Development, Report No. 11, September 1978, 104 pp., original Dutch.

6 WORLD FOOD PROBLEMS AND THE NEW INTERNATIONAL ECONOMIC ORDER

Antoine J. Groosman

6.1. INTRODUCTION

With a considerable part of the world population on the verge
of starvation and an increasing number of people suffering
from malnutrition and undernourishment, food production and
distribution are two of the most urgent problems in the international community.

The food problem, in terms of production and distribution, is
an international problem affecting hundreds of millions of
people living in Third World countries. Recent estimates of
the number of people suffering from hunger and malnutrition
vary from half a billion to one and a half billion, depending
on the methodology of setting the minimum requirements of basic food needs. The FAO estimate of a figure of 500 million
hungry and malnourished people is the most generally accepted
approximation. According to the Director-General of the FAO
the greater part of the world's population suffers absolute
poverty. (1)
A billion people are at the lowest levels of existence, lacking in one or more of the basic needs; enough food and drinking water, adequate housing and minimum hygiene. These figures
point to the fact that the world food problem is immense and
that a solution within the foreseeable future seems unrealistic and impossible. In Africa, Asia and Latin America many
countries are not yet in a position to feed the poor people
from their own soils and resources.

Food aid for these countries has become a structural phenomenon, while, in fact, food aid was only meant and justified as
a temporary instrument to overcome serious food shortages. The
annual target of food aid pledged for was still nearly 10 million tons in 1977; this compares with nearly 12 million tons
during the world food crisis five years ago.

It is generally accepted that the food situation will deterio-
rate even more in the future if growth and distribution continue as forecast to the year 2000. Unless effective action
occurs at the international level, food problems will be more
pressing then than they are today.

In this paper we will describe, at first, the past, current
and expected trend in food production and trade, with special
attention to the least developed and most seriously affected
countries; the LLDC's and MSA countries respectively. (2) In
these countries hunger and starvation are most pronounced.

Next, because production and trade of basic foodstuffs are becoming more and more "internationalized", we will assess the
possibilities of solving international food problems within
the framework of international institutions (U.N. agencies)
and briefly analyze the role of multinational enterprises and
lending agencies in agricultural development in Third World
countries. In particular, we will remark on the question of
whether or not a strategy of the establishment of a New International Economic Order, as adopted by the United Nations
General Assembly at its Sixth Special Session in April/May
1974, opened new perspectives in solving international food
problems and will give concrete scope to improving the standard of living of the hundreds of millions of hungry and malnourished people in Third World countries.

Finally, we will make some concluding remarks on the future
of world food production and trade and on the specific role of
the agriculture of Third World countries in an international
framework.

6.2. FOOD PRODUCTION AND DISTRIBUTION IN THIRD WORLD COUNTRIES

Farming techniques in many of the developing countries have
remained almost unchanged for centuries. Yields per hectare
and per farmer are very low compared to industrialized nations. In the last two decades, however, modern farming techniques were introduced in some selected parts of the Third
World. In this section we will analyze the impact of modern
farming techniques on food production and trade.

First we will briefly outline the trends in food production and distribution in developing countries over the last
decades.

6.2.1. Food production and trade in developing countries

It is difficult to make an analysis of food production and
distribution in the developing countries as a group because
agricultural development and production differ from region to
region and from country to country as well as within countries
themselves. Therefore, we will distinguish between the very
poor countries (LLDC's and MSA countries) and other developing
countries (OPEC countries and countries summarized in the
table in Annex 2). Food problems are most pronounced in the

first group of countries. A common characteristic of these
countries is a very low per capita income and the importance
of agriculture in the economy.

In the least developed countries, for instance, industrial
activities contribute less than 10 percent to the Gross National Product. For the MSA countries as a group, agriculture
provides employment for up to almost 70 percent of the total
population and makes up 40 percent of the Gross National Product. In LLDC's these figures are still higher.

The LLCD's and MSA countries are mainly situated in Africa
South of the Sahara and in the Far East and Pacific regions.
As far as food consumption is concerned all these countries,
fifty nations, are substantial net importers of basic foodstuffs, relying on food aid and commercial food imports from
industrialized countries (see Annex 1).

During the period of 1961-1974 the annual growth of food production in the least-developed and MSA countries was significantly lower than annual population growth, resulting in
stagnant or declining per capita food supplies.

In fact, some of these countries (such as Guyana, Mali,
Kampuchea), traditionally in a position to export cereals,
have become importers of basic foodstuffs in the 1970's.
Agricultural imports in the MSA countries, as a group, increased not only in terms of value, but also in terms of volume.

Cereals imported in these countries rose by about 2 million tons in 1974; production declined by 14 million tons.
During the last two years in many Third World countries, good
crops have been harvested. But good production figures have
not been registered in all poor countries. In Africa and in
the poorest food-deficit countries, the food situation is
still precarious and unsatisfactory. Dependence on food aid has
not diminished.

In Table 1 (see also Annex 1 and 2) net imports of cereals in
all developing regions are summarized for the period of 1934/
1938-1976. Some net-exporting regions in the developing world
became net-importing after the Second World War, especially,
as just pointed out, countries with MSA and LLDC status in
Africa and Asia.

Table 1

Cereal importing and exporting regions in the world
1934/1938-1976 (in millions of tons)

Region Year	1934/38	1948/52	1960	1966	1973	1976
N.America	+ 5	+ 22	+ 39	+ 59	+ 91	+ 97
W.Europe	- 24	- 22	- 25	- 27	- 19	- 25
E.Europe (USSR)	+ 5	0	0	- 4	- 27	- 29
Australia/ New Zealand	+ 3	+ 3	+ 6	+ 6	+ 6	+ 3
Latin America (1)	+ 9	+ 1	0	+ 5	- 3	- 1
Africa	+ 1	0	- 2	- 7	- 5	- 7
Asia (2)	+ 3	- 6	- 17	- 34	- 43	- 46

Sources: L. Brown/E.Eckholm; By bread alone, Praeger, New
         York, 1974.
         Trade Yearbook, 1976, FAO, Rome

(1) Cereal exports of Argentina amounted to 10 million tons
    in 1976.

(2) Including Japanese imports (29 million tons in 1976), ex-
    cluding China, Thai rice exports amounted to 4.4 million
    tons in 1976.

- = net-importer
+ = net-exporter

In other developing countries (3), which are in a process of
industrialization or have rich natural resources (for instance the OPEC countries), agriculture is often in a more advanced stage of development. Although modern farm techniques have
been introduced in these countries, the majority of them are
not able, up to now, to more or less achieve self-sufficiency
in basic food production.

Indonesia, the Philippines, Malaysia, South Korea, Iran,
countries in Latin America (except Argentina) and countries
north of the Sahara, for instance, are substantial net-import-
ers of basic foodstuffs. These countries, however, are in a
position to buy grains and other foodstuffs in international
markets, because they have substantial foreign currency obtained by exporting raw materials, agricultural produce or
(semi-) industrial products. For the future it is foreseen
that more developing countries will succeed in selling industrial products to industrialized countries (4), increasing the
purchasing power of these countries.

On the other hand, developing countries in the group 'other
developing countries' will have to import enormous quantities

of agricultural requisites and machinery to modernize their agricultures. Imports of fertilizers, pesticides and tractors have increased, in terms of value and volume, at high growth rates, whereas food imports have not fallen over the last decade. Table 2 shows net-imports of cereals, fertilizer, pesticides and tractors into all developing countries. The 'Green Revolution', as we will see, requires more for success than just planting new seeds; these seeds need sufficient plant nutrients and controlled water supplies, requisites that are often beyond the financial reach of small and medium-small farmers in developing regions (see 6.2.2.).

Table 2

Net-imports of cereals and means of agricultural production by developing countries (in millions of U.S. dollars), excl. China

Year	Cereals	Fertilizer	Pesticides	Tractors	Total
1968	2,420	693	201	354	3,668
1969	2,039	555	231	388	3,213
1970	2,420	509	269	405	3,603
1971	2,661	561	270	445	3,937
1972	2,585	756	305	495	4,141
1973	5,468	1,186	460	587	7,701
1974	9,301	2,537	655	809	13,302
1975	9,655	3,016	809	1,155	14,635
1976	8,287	--	--	--	--

Source: FAO, Trade Yearbook, 1973 and 1976, Rome.

In more advanced developing countries, in terms of income per capita, we can observe that imports of 'luxury' dairy products rose considerably in the 1970's. These imports are concentrated in oil-producing and exporting countries having high incomes per capita. Table 3 provides some data on imports of milkpowder, condensed milk, butter and cheese by developing countries. The share of OPEC countries in total imports of developing countries for these products are 30, 48, 35 and 55 percent respectively.

Table 3

Imports of dairy products by Third World countries (in thousands of tons), 1970/73-1976

	Year	Milk-powder	Condensed milk	Butter	Cheese
Oil-exporting	'70/'73	142	137	34	24
Developing	1975	146	198	59	48
Countries	1976	238	230	77	67
All develop-ing countries	'70/'73	616	443	173	83
	1975	600	440	192	103
Oil-exporting countries as	1976	850	475	215	125
% total imports	1976	30	48	35	55

Source: International dairy situation and outlook and implications for dairy development in developing countries,
FAO, Rome, 19-7-1977.

The dairy products, although rich in proteins and vitamins,
mostly, are far beyond the reach of the poorest groups within OPEC countries and in relatively more advanced developing
nations. It is quite obvious that the short availability of
good clear drinking water is a constraint to fully exploiting
the benefits of milkpowder. As overproduction of dairy products in Western countries becomes more manifest, imports of
'luxury' dairy products by developed nations (5) will, however, increase considerably.

It is now recognized that if the people of the poorest countries are to be fed, the food will have to come to a large extent from their own farmers, their own resources and their
farm economies.
     Up to now, however, few of the developing nations mention-
ed above recognized that food independence is a national or
regional affair and that if agricultural development is giv-
en priority, the basis for improving an entire economy is
laid. Such development policy can eliminate food problems in
developing countries in the longer run. By investing in agriculture, a greater output is within the reach of many developing nations with vast potentialities to reclaim as yet unex-
ploited and underexploited land which, put into practical use,
would considerably contribute to the solution of food problems. Another way of attaining a level of sufficient growth
in basic food production in developing countries is intensification of production on already cultivated land. Especially
in Asian countries, where the man/land ratio is very high and
expansion of arable land is rather limited, intensification
of production per hectare is one of the great potentials for
improving the world food situation. In 1974 the United Nations Research Institute for Social Development (UNRISD) (6)

calculated that the number of unviable or uneconomic holdings in Asia may come to about 80 million, or some 80 percent of all holdings. Asia would need an additional area of 112 million hectares (about 250 million acres) to bring holdings to an average level of 2.5 hectares each. The total area held under holdings above 20 hectares is only 42 million hectares. Asia is indeed the world's most vulnerable region in food production. In the near future hunger on a nationwide scale is possible in South Asia; from Pakistan to India, Bangladesh and Java and from the Philippines to Sri Lanka.

Some observers (7) state, however, that small farmers in Asia can make a decent living on two acres (0.8 hectares) with the use of fertilizers, water and high-yielding seeds.

Without these inputs, and this is still by far the reality in great parts of Asia, a farmer would need ten acres (4.0 hectares). Where new techniques in agriculture are introduced, multiple cropping of two or three crops on the same piece of land is possible. Yields, as a result, are then much larger than traditional ones. Intensification of agriculture is not a new strategy in developing countries where land and capital are scarce, but has been stimulated by international agencies since the 1960's.

The effects of 'modernizing' agricultures in developing countries on food production and distribution in the last two decades were, however, not sufficient to solve the world food problem or to diminish the number of people in Third World countries suffering from hunger and malnutrition. A brief analysis of the Green Revolution is given below.

6.2.2. Disillusionment with the 'Green Revolution'

The Green Revolution, based on high-yielding grain varieties requiring controlled water supplies, sufficient fertilizer, and, where necessary, pesticides, was introduced in the rural areas of Third World countries in the 1960's. Compared to traditional farming practices, the production of basic food in developing countries under the Green Revolution strategy required much more capital and technology.

Initially, the new farming methods led to a massive increase of imports of agricultural requisites in developing countries and to a 'technology transfer' from developed to developing countries.

In some Third World countries, where capital was concentrated by the big farmers, capital was channelled into the production of cereals. The advantage of the so-called Green Revolution was that attention and publicity was concentrated on rural development. Before the new farming practices were introduced, rural development was one of the most neglected areas. At the end of the 1960's we could observe that in some developing countries grain production increased at a fast rate.

A few countries (Mexico and Pakistan, for instance) were even

in a position to export cereals, although this is not very
surprising because of the rather small commercial internal
market in developing countries. Nevertheless, good crops were
harvested in large parts of the Third World. Good weather
conditions and relatively low input prices (in particular fertilizer prices) also contributed to increased production at
the end of the 1960's. Initially, the Green Revolution had a
positive effect on food production in Third World countries.

In the early and mid-1970's the success of the Green Revolution as regards food production was largely erased because of
adverse weather conditions, high input prices of fuel, fertilizer and pesticides and relatively low prices of agricultural produce. Under the Green Revolution mode of production it
is clear that yield increments, in terms of money, must be
set against the cost of additional inputs before the profit-
ability of high-yielding seed can be assessed.
   Table 4 provides some data on cost/benefit relations in
paddy production in four countries for the years 1970 and 1974.
Fertilizer (N-urea) application is taken as the only input.

Table 4

Prices paid by farmers for fertilizer and prices received by
farmers for paddy in four selected countries in 1970 and 1974
(prices in U.S. cents per kg.)

	1970			1974		
	paddy	N urea	paddy N	paddy	N urea	paddy N
Sri Lanka	11.3	15.0	0.75	22.6	60.1	0.38
Philippines	5.6	21.3	0.26	12.6	51.9	0.24
Japan	30.8	22.1	1.39	60.3	42.6	1.42
U.S.A.	11.4	19.9	0.57	30.9	39.1	0.80

Source: IRRI, World Rice Statistics, April 1977.

As we can see from Table 4 the price relation between paddy and
fertilizer in developing countries, in this case Sri Lanka and
the Philippines, is very unprofitable compared with the same
relation for rice producers in the U.S.A. and Japan. In 1970,
when fertilizer prices where low (in the case of Sri Lanka the
fertilizer price for 1970 is a subsidized price) cost/benefit
relations in developing countries were already unfavourable.
This situation deteriorated enormously in the mid-1970's, especially in regions where serious inequalities (social and
economic) already existed.
   Small farmers, then, were not in a position to buy enough
inputs.

In general, the introduction of new varieties of grain and
modern farm-systems led to an increase in productivity for a

limited group of farmers, having superior endowments (in terms of land and capital) and social status, while the majority of poor people (8) were partially excluded from the benefits of increased productivity.

Thus, the introduction of modern inputs and technology had gone hand in hand with the further concentration of wealth among the already "wealthy" people in those regions.

The small farmer, however, can accept the modern technology only rather slowly or not at all, because the innovations are too risky and not profitable on his small plot. Fluctuations in input and output prices and low prices for his crop do not give him sufficient incentive to reap the full benefit of the Green Revolution strategy.

It is important to emphasize that an adverse impact of the use of new seeds, fertilizer and farm implements on development comes not from the Green Revolution itself, but more from the social-economic structures into which the technology is introduced.

Therefore, in countries with no great inequalities in rural areas, the technology based on modern inputs can make a substantial contribution to agricultural development and the solving of food problems (an example of such a country is the People's Republic of China).

An additional constraint to rural development in developing countries with market-economies, was that women's role in agriculture was greatly underestimated during the introduction of modern farming techniques. (9) Now it is recognized that the majority of women in the Third World's agricultures did not benefit from the new farming practices. Women, for instance, had earned in the past a steady income from weeding of fields, which they did as a part-time activity. The Green Revolution (10) took away this source of income for rural female labourers in many countries because improved agriculture was associated with modern inputs like chemicals for weed removal. Chemical spraying is rather capital intensive and this work is done by male labour.

We come to the conclusion that the Green Revolution, initially, led to a substantial increase in land productivity and food production in some selected parts of Third World countries. The diffusion of modern farm techniques, however, did not reach the majority of the poorest groups. On the one hand, small and medium-small farmers were not in a position to buy enough seeds and fertilizers at reasonable prices and at the right time of the cropping season, while on the other hand, the unemployment of landless labourers (male but in particular female) increased substantially in rural areas in Third World countries. (11)

It may be more rational for Third World countries to at first increase existing and new sources of employment by using labour intensive techniques and modern farm inputs such as high-yielding seeds and fertilizer. Such innovations will lead to a decline of unemployment in rural areas because increased production will require more labour. In the process of change, measures to improve credit facilities, marketing systems, infrastructure, training and technical assistance are unavoidable complements for successful rural development. Furthermore, increased food production can also create employment in input supplying and food processing industries.

After this process of development, more sophisticated technologies in agriculture based on more expensive farm implements (tractors, combine harvesters and the like) may become desirable.

6.2.3. Food security and national policies in Third World countries

In 1976 and 1977 grain production in developing countries increased sharply, although the situation in Africa and some food deficit countries is still unsatisfactory. In fact, on a world scale, grain production could, at present, more than adequately feed every person on earth. Even during the 'scarcity' period, 1972/1973, there was 9 percent more grain per person than in an 'ample' year like 1960.

Distribution over supplies, however, is very unequal in the world, especially in developing countries with large income disparities. There is in these countries no guarantee that the poorest groups, even in years of good harvests, will have enough te eat. It seems that the real issue is not the quantity of food, but who grows it and who has how much money to buy it. (12)

In inegalitarian countries it is difficult to change the income structure. Growth in such countries can easily go hand in hand with greater hunger and falling incomes for the poorest members of the society. Low agricultural prices for basic foodstuffs in developing countries are favourable, for instance,for urban groups but for the rural farmers they are a disincentive to grow these basic foodstuffs.

In Brazil, for instance, seven out of eight of the country's eleven million farmers receive no loans at all, as a result of a low repayment capacity. (13) Yet these farmers provide most of the rice, beans, maize and cassave for Brazil's population. Only the richest farmers, growing export-crops (coffee and soybeans) have access to government loans. Developing countries recognized that the great price/volume fluctuations on international markets for export crops also have a negative impact on agricultural development and securing national food supplies.

Striving after a 'New International Economic Order', as we will see in 6.3.2. can have a substantial impact on the strengthening of the purchasing power of these countries. Therefore, more stable prices, a higher level of prices and increased control over production of primary agricultural commodities are necessary in order for developing countries to

formulate policies regarding food security within their countries.

Because national policies in developing countries with open
market economies are greatly influenced by international developments, it is necessary to solve food problems in an international framework. The success of international arrangements on prices and production, therefore, are a prerequisite
to the fullfilment of development plans in developing countries as regards national food security. The distribution of
benefits, from possible new international arrangements, within developing countries, towards the poorest groups, will be
one of the greatest challenges for these countries themselves.

6.2.4. Food and international relations

North America since the Second World War, has become the leading exporter of cereals in the world. In 1976 the United States and Canada had a surplus of almost 100 million tons of cereals (see Table 1).

These two countries, in particular the United States, export
large quantities of cereals to developing countries and in
fact are in a position to dominate the world markets of cereals.

Hundreds of millions of people in developing countries have to
rely on the American breadbasket. The 'dependence' of developing countries on U.S. grain supplies is by far a result of the
food aid programmes of rich countries or food exports on easily negotiated concessional terms. The disposing of surplusses
by developed countries has kept prices in developing countries
low at levels at which local farmers have no incentive to produce more basic foodstuffs.

Table 4, for instance, showed that Philippines' farmers receive very low prices for paddy. The Philippines in the past
received food imports from U.S. sources in great quantities
(in 1963-1967 and 1971-1974) at concessional terms. These imports, as one of the major components, kept prices for Philippines' farmers verly low and as a result they shifted to more
profitable export crops (sugar).

Increasing dependence on food and agricultural requisites (see
Table 2) imported by many developing countries from rich countries is also a structural constraint to becoming self-suffic-
ient in basic foodstuffs. Therefore, it is necessary that food
problems, more and more becoming international problems, be
solved within an international framework.

In the past, in order to stabilize prices and earnings for
agricultural commodities,international arrangements came into
existence. For wheat, sugar, coffee and cocoa such arrangements were negotiated between producing and consuming countries. It now seems necessary, however, to revise these ar-

rangements because prices, supplies and earnings still fluctuate enormously over years. The strenghtening of the purchasing power of developing countries by existing commodity arrangements has been almost negligible. Where increased prices
for the agricultural exports of developing countries were negotiated, these increases were largely wiped out by increased
input prices for agricultural requisites.

In the early 1970's, developing countries became more aware
of the widening gap between themselves and developed countries in a system (the 'economic order') which was established
at a time when most of the developing countries were colonies
and which perpetuates inequality between 'rich' and 'poor'
countries.

The process of awareness of the disadvantages in the 'old
order' resulted in demands for a 'new order' in which particular attention should be given to the taking of effective
measures by the international community to assist the developing countries in overcoming the continuing severe economic
imbalances in the relations between these countries and developed nations.

As regards food problems we will, next, outline what was 'new'
in the New International Economic Order and assess the effects
of possible new international arrangements for primary agricultural commodities for developing nations.

6.3. WORLD FOOD PROBLEMS AND THE NEW INTERNATIONAL ECONOMIC
     ORDER

The demands for new rules in international economic relations
resulted at the Sixth Special Session of the United Nations
in April/May 1974 in the adoption of the Declaration on the
Establishment of a New International Economic Order.

The NIEO Declaration aims at revising the rules of international economic relations in order to provide more equal possibilities to all governments, in developing as well as developed countries. The NIEO deals with a multitude of economic issues such as commodity price stabilization and support,
indexation, the Common Fund, the Integrated Commodity Programme, debt relief programmes, Special Drawing Rights, trade
liberalization, trade preferences and transfer of technologies.
     A 'programme' dealing exclusively with food production and
trade was adopted at the Sixth Special Session. An abstract
of this 'programme' is given in Annex 3. Although the effects
of all above-mentioned issues on world food production and
trade may be substantial, we mainly focus here on the possible effects of the 'Food Programme' of the New International
Economic Order.
     This 'Food Programme of Action' was partially discussed at
the World Food Conference in November 1974, where the FAO con-

ference called for the creation of three <u>new international</u>
<u>bodies</u>:
- the World Food Council, a body of representatives from mi-
  nistries of agriculture in 36 nations (WFC),
- the Consultative Group on Food Production and Investment,
- the International Fund for Agricultural Development (IFAD).

6.3.1. What is 'New' in the New International Economic Order
       as regards food production and trade?

One of the most important objectives of the New International
Economic Order in respect to world food production and trade
is to facilitate the transfer of food and agricultural inputs
between developed and underdeveloped countries. A New International Economic Order would eliminate conditions imposed on
these transfers and ensure that developing countries can import the necessary quantities of food without undue strain on
their foreign exchange resources and without inpredictable deterioration in their balance of payments. Special measures
should be taken in respect of LLDC's and MSA countries.

'New' in the programme of action on food problems is that developed countries will ensure an increase in all available inputs, including fertilizers, <u>on favourable terms</u> to increase
food production in developing countries. Up to now, imports of
agricultural inputs by developing nations showed fluctuating,
temporary and excessively high price-levels, hindering a
necessary increase of agricultural production in developing
countries. (14)

'Old' priorities in the New International Economic Order as
regards food production and trade are:
- promoting exports of food and non-food crops of developing
  countries through just and equitable arrangements,
- increasing food storage facilities in developing countries,
- arresting desertification, salination and damage by natural
  disasters and pests in developing countries,
- increasing food aid in times of food shortages,
- increasing agricultural land, which is not yet exploited or
  underexploited.

The United Nations Programme of Action on these priorities
does not differ considerably from food programmes formulated
and adopted by the Food and Agriculture Organization (FAO) and
the World Bank. Again, emphasis is laid on ensuring that concrete measures will be made to increase production in developing countries and that agricultural growth will reach farmers
in the Third World's rural areas.
   We can, however, observe an evolution in thinking within
the concerned international organizations. Whereas in the early 1970's emphasis was given to growth within Third World's
agricultures now the question is added: for whose benefit is
this increased production and agricultural growth?
   A consensus has been reached that production and distribution policies must be fully integrated. The World Bank's Mahbub

ul Haq (15) says that there is now broad agreement on certain
propositions which would have been regarded as heresies only
a decade ago:
- Growth in the GNP often does not filter down. What is needed is a direct attack on mass poverty.
- Policies to improve the distribution of benefits and employment opportunities must be an integral part of any production plan. It is generally impossible to produce first and
  distribute later.
- A vital element in distribution policies is to increase the
  productivity of the poor by directing investment toward
  them.
- A drastic restructuring of political and economic power is
  often required if development is to spread to the vast majority of the population.
- The market mechanism is often distorted by the existing distribution of income and wealth in favour of the rich, and is
  generally an unreliable guide in setting national objectives. Reforming existing institutions is usually more decisive
  than modifying prices to benefit the poor.
- New development strategies must be aimed at the satisfaction
  of the basic human needs of the entire population rather
  than at fulfilling market demand.

These changing policies of international organizations as regards the poorest groups in developing countries do not stress
explicitly the new international rules which would overcome
economic inequalities between developed and underdeveloped
nations. It is, however, recognized that structural barriers
in international relations have had a negative effect on food
production and distribution in Third World countries.

International markets for grains, for instance, have been very
'cyclical' (as a result of the fluctioning of the market mechanism) in the past. Since the 1950's the cyclical appearance
of excessive and short supplies has been a permanent market
feature. Despite the Wheat Agreements since 1949 prices have
not been stable and security over supplies (buffer stocks) has
not been guaranteed.
    The only achievement in the 1971-1974 International Grains
Agreement was the maintenance of an institutional frame for
international communication in wheat matters and the assurance
of a basic food-aid contribution amounting to 4.3 million tons.

This year a new agreement should come into operation, but up
to now (16) delegates from major wheat importing and exporting countries have been unable to reach agreements on the text
for a new International Wheat Agreement. Possible production
cuts are strongly objected to by consuming countries, whereas
disagreement on the size of the stocks also exists between
consumers and producers.

In a new International Wheat Agreement,cereal-importing developing countries will want the securing of supplies for import requirements at the best possible terms (e.g. stabiliza-

tion of world market prices, reserve stocks for emergencies, etc.)

Grain exporters, mainly U.S. multinational enterprises, have a substantial power in internal grain markets and the U.S. food supplies and surplusses, for example, provide 'virtual life and death power over the fate of the multitudes of needy people'. (17) Grain, as the basic foodstuff of the world's population, is a strategic product in the establishment of the New International Economic Order. As a result it will be necessary for international institutions (the United Nations) to negotiate directly with multinational enterprises dominating distribution of basic foodstuffs in order to solve world food problems in an international framework.

According to Gonzalo Arroyo (18) there may be a conflict between international institutions and multinationals in the establishment of a NIEO. The structuring of a NIEO, as stipulated by the United Nations, may not necessarily coincide with the structuring of a 'New International Economic Order' for agriculture led by multinational enterprises and their subsidiaries. Arroyo says that 'national economies [of both industrial and Third World countries] are integrated in a world system in different ways and at different speeds, depending on the previous degree of capitalization of industry and other economic sectors; the availability, cost and training of the labour, the abundance of natural resources and the nature of stability of political and social institutions in each country'.

Therefore, it is possible that a greater number of countries with no substantial resources, small markets (in terms of purchasing power) and no access to funds will be 'excluded' from the process of development and from the possible effects of the New International Economic Order. In international economic development, most of the Least Developed and Most Seriously Affected countries will probably be ignored. These countries will be more or less left to their fate or will become increasingly dependent on foreign aid.

As regards food production, it is by no means certain that, in the striving after the establishment of a NIEO, developing countries will benefit from more basic-food production in the world. It is, for instance, quite possible that the 'rich' developed nations will absorb a great part of the additional cereal production in the world by increasing meat and milk production.

6.3.2. Scope for improving the world food situation under the
       New International Economic Order

The scope for improving the Third World's food situation can be broadened substantially by developing agricultures within the developing countries themselves. Rural development within developing countries, however, is only possible by the removal

of national and international constraints to the production
of more food and other crops.

The most important constraint in international relations as
regards rural development and food production in Third World
countries is the lack of purchasing power of the rural masses
to 'modernize' their farming techniques. Although traditional
farming is still very important in large parts of rural Africa and Asia it will be necessary, for the future, to increase
yields. Otherwise a decent living in the rural areas cannot
be guaranteed for the majority of poor farmers.

In order to 'modernize' agricultures in Third World countries
the Programme of Action of the United Nations to establish a
NIEO opens some new perspectives.

A prerequisite to improving agricultural development in Third
World countries, however, is that on the one hand the input-
supplying industries (producers of fertilizer pesticides and
farm implements) can guarantee full access to supplies at
reasonable prices and that, on the other, food-processing industries pay more stable prices for primary agricultural commodities.
    To accelerate the export earnings, measures have to be
taken which affect prices and volume of the agricultural commodities.

International agreements on inputs and outputs as regards food
and non-food production, therefore, can be negotiated within
the framework of a New International Economic Order. The possible benefits of new agreements on agricultural inputs and commodities will accrue, initially, to nation states, export organizations, producers' associations or (multinational) private
enterprises.
    One of the major problems, distributing the accrued benefits
of nation states to the poorest people (farmers, landless farmers and tenants), however, cannot be solved within an international framework, but it seems quite possible to improve the
conditions of the rural masses by international action.

In short the new perspectives within a NIEO for agricultural
development within Third World countries are:
- to fully secure access to input supplies of developed as well
  as developing countries at reasonable prices,
- to accelerate export earnings for the agricultural primary
  commodities of Third World countries through higher and favourable prices and through controlling output,
- to transfer appropriate farming techniques to developing
  countries with the aim of stimulating basic foodstuff production,
- to increase food aid in particular to vulnerable groups
  (children) and countries,
- to improve food storage capacity in developing countries,
- to stimulate and finance fertilizer production and distribution in developing countries.

At the moment there is great frustration and resentment in the Third World at the lack of progress in creating a NIEO (19), even though IFAD (the International Fund for Agricultural Development) was agreed upon in June 1976 with a subscription of $1 billion by Western countries and members of OPEC.

Furthermore, Arab countries have established an Arab Authority for Agricultural Investment and Development with a six-year plan for investing $2.8 billion in rural development in the Middle East, with particular attention to developing the resources of southern Sudan. Sudan is potentially one of the richest farming regions in the world, with enough resources to produce enormous quantities of food.

Here it is, again, important to recognize that world food problems are not only a result of limitations on potential output but are founded in social and political structures of nations and in the economic relations among countries.

6.4. CONCLUDING REMARKS

The strategy of developing countries to establish new international economic rules (the purpose of a New International Economic Order) can create a basis for reducing economic inequalities in trade between nations, because a framework is thereby created to negotiate on food and related problems.

It seems not likely, however, that the establishment of a New International Economic Order will be possible within the next two decades; this is because of the economic power of food and fertilizer exporting nations and multinational trading companies. What can be done in the foreseeable future is to improve agricultural development within Third World countries themselves, with great emphasis on a satisfactory degree of self-sufficiency in basic food production.

The stimulation of indigenous food production and adequate distribution of food to the poorest groups will be necessary in ensuing years; it is evident that a country that is dependent on world food markets has no guaranteee of solving its food problems.

FOOTNOTES

1. Statement by Edouard Saouma to the Nineteenth Session of the FAO-Conference, c77/LIM/1, 1977 November, 1977.

2. In August 1974 the United Nations gave 32 developing countries the status of most seriously affected (MSA countries). Ten more countries were added to the list between December 1974 and May 1975. Recently the number increased to 45. The MSA countries and Least Developed Countries (LLDC's) together constitute a group of 50 countries (see Annex 1).

3. Summarized in Annex 2 (only for countries with a population of over 10 million people).

4. See chapter 5: "International Industrial Relocation; Some Factors of Change", by Ben H. Evers.

5. The danger of 'dumping' these products can become a real constraint to developing production in Third World countries.

6. Rao, V., Growth with justice in Asian agricultures, UNRISD, 1974.

7. "Revolution it isn't but it can be green for everyone", The Economist, 13 May 1978.

8. Small farmers, landless farmers, tenant-owners and sub-marginal farmers.

9. Devake Jain, "Women are separate", in Development Forum, August 1978.

10. A completely western technological invention.

11. According to Andrew Pearse (UNRISD) the tractor roughly reduces labour requirements per crop to the same extent that the new technology increased them. Introduction of tractor-powered dispersal of weedicide and fertilizer, aerial spraying and the use of harvesters cuts back the labour force very radically. Andrew Pearse "Technology and Peasant Production: Reflections of a Global Study", in: Development and Change, 8 (1977), p. 149.

12. "World Grain; Plenty", The Economist, August 19, 1978, p. 61.

13. "You cannot eat cheap loans", The Economist, May 8, 1978, p. 8.

14. Vingerhoets, J. and Groosman, A.: The Western European fertilizer industry and the Third World; national cartels, export

cartels and the residual market, Development Research Institute, Tilburg, December 1977. (in Dutch and English).

15. Mahbub ul Haq; in Finance and Development, June 1978,
Volume 15/number 2.

16. "Wheat Talks Faltering", in ISCA News 6:78, June 1978. The
International Wheat Agreement of 1974 expired on 30 June
1978.

17. In: "What now", Dag Hammarsköld Report, 1975.

18. Gonzalo Arroyo, Institutional Constraints to Policies for
Achieving Increased Food Production in Selected Countries,
Rome, 1976.

19. Statement by E. Saouma, Nineteenth Session of the FAO Conference, November 1977, Rome. C77/LIM/lp3.

REFERENCES

United Nations World Food Conference - Assessment of the
World Food Situation, Present and Future; FAO, Rome, 1974.

The State of Food and Agriculture, FAO, Rome (annually
issued).

The World Food Problem: Proposals for National and International Action, UN-FAO, mimeo, Rome, 1974.

The World Food Situation and Prospects to 1985, USDA, Washington D.C., 1974.

The Stabilization of International Trade in Grains; an Assessment of Problems and Possible Solutions, FAO, Rome, 1975.

Study of Trends in World Supply and Demand of Major Agricultural Commodities, OECD, Paris, 1976.

McNamara, R., One Hundred Countries, Two Billion People; The
Dimensions of Development, Preager Publishers, New York,
1973.

Assault on World Poverty, IBRD, John Hopkins University Press,
Baltimore, 1975.

Mahbub ul Haq, The Third World and The International Economic
Order, Overseas Development Council, Washington D.C., 1976.

"Towards a Rational and Equitable New International Economic
Order: a Case for Negotiated Structural Changes", in: World
Development, Vol. 3, no. 6, June 1975.

"The World Food Problem: Consensus and Conflict", in: World
Development, Vol. 5, no. 5-7, May-July 1977.

"Increased Stability of Grain Supplies in Developing Countries: optimal carryovers and insurance", in: World Development, Vol. 4, no. 12, December 1976.

Brandt, Hartmut, A New International Grains Agreement - Problems and Approaches for Solution, German Development Institute, Berlin, 1976.

Matzke, O., "Nährung als weltpolitisches Machtsinstrument",
in: Europa Archiv, no. 5, 1977.

Radetzki, M., International Commodity Marketing Arrangements,
London, 1970.

Linnemann, H., J. de Hoogh, M. Keyzer and H. van Heemst,
MOIRA - A Model of International Relations in Agriculture,
Report of the Project Group 'Food for a Growing World Population; North-Holland Publishing Company, Amsterdam,
1978.

Reshaping the International Order, RIO-Report to the Club of
Rome, New York, 1976.

Hopper, D., "The Development of Agriculture in Developing
Countries", in: Scientific American, Vol. 235, no. 3, September 1976.

Griffin, Keith, The Green Revolution: an Economic Analysis,
UNRISD, Genève, 1974.

Jacoby, E. and C., Man and Land: The Fundamental Issue in Development, London, 1974.

ANNEX 1

Least Developed Countries (LLDC's) and Most Seriously Affected (MSA) Countries in 1977

Country	LLDC status (1)	MSA status	Population (in mill.) 1976	GDP per capita in US $ 1976	Net cereal imports (x 1000 ton) 1975
Benin	x	x	3,2	130	30
Burundi	x	x	3,8	120	10
Botswana	x	.	0,7	410	35
Central African Empire (CEA)	x	x	1,8	230	17
Egypt	.	x	28,0	280	3,165
Ethiopia	x	x	28,6	100	16
Gambia	x	x	0,5	180	50
Ghana	.	x	10,1	580	162
Guinea	x	x	5,7	150	40
Guinee Bissau	.	x	0,5	140	20
Ivory Coast	.	x	7,0	610	108
Cape Verde Islands (2)	.	x	0,3	260	28
Cameroon	.	x	7,6	290	73
Kenya	.	x	13,8	240	− 100
Lesotho	x	x	1,2	170	50
Madagascar	.	x	9,1	200	113
Malawi	x	.	5,2	140	36
Mali	x	x	5,8	100	59
Mauratania	.	x	1,3	340	137
Mozambique	.	x	9,5	170	214
Niger	x	x	4,7	160	69
Uganda	x	x	11,9	240	17
Upper Volta	x	x	6,2	110	37
Rwanda	x	x	4,2	110	9
Senegal	.	x	5,1	390	278
Sierra Leone	.	x	3,0	200	45
Sudan	x	x	15,9	290	175
Somalia	x	x	3,3	110	111
Tanzania	x	x	15,1	180	97
Chad	x	x	4,1	120	19
Afghanistan	x	x	14,0	160	13
Bangladesh	x	x	80,4	110	1,470
Bhutan	x	.	1,2	70	1
Burma	.	x	30,8	120	− 586
Yemen (North)	x	x	1,7	280	110
Yemen (South)	x	x	6,0	250	344
India	.	x	620,4	150	6,489
Kampuchea (2)	.	x	8,2	−	21
Laos	x	x	3,3	90	. 121
Maldives	x	.	0,1	110	6
Nepal	x	x	12,9	120	− 13
Pakistan	.	x	71,3	170	403
Sikkim	x	.	−	−	11
Sri Lanka	.	x	13,8	200	926
West Samoa	x	x	0,2	350	7
El Salvador	.	x	4,1	490	104
Guatemala	.	x	6,5	630	157
Guyana	.	x	0,8	540	3
Haïti	x	x	4,7	200	104
Honduras	.	x	3,0	390	107

Source: World Bank Atlas, 1977

(1) The criteria for Least Developed Countries (LLDC's) were identified by the UN in 1971:
    - GDP per capita was 100 $ (US) or less (revised),
    - the share of manufacturing 10 percent or less,
    - literacy-rate of 20 percent or less of population aged 15 years and more.
    These criteria were applied with some flexibility in marginal cases.

(2) 1975.

ANNEX 2

Other developing countries, population over 10 million inhabitants, cereals imported 1975 (net-figures and GDP)

Country	Population 1976 (x million)	GDP per capita 1976 (US $)	Net-cereal imports (1) 1975 (x 1000 ton)
China, People's Republic of	836,8	410	2,624
Indonesia	135,2	240	2,351
Vietnam	47,6	n.a.	1,778
Philippines	43,3	410	901
Thailand	43,0	380	− 4,278
Turkey	41,2	990	24
Korea (South)	40,0	670	2,783
Iran	34,3	1.930	1,639
Taiwan	16,3	1.070	n.a.
Korea (North)	16,2	470	70
Malaysia	12,6	860	980
Iraq	11,5	1.390	682
Brazil	110,0	1.140	995
Mexico	62,0	1.090	998
Argentina	25,7	1.550	− 10,155
Colombia	24,4	630	252
Peru	15,8	800	1,146
Venezuela	12,4	2.570	1,804
Chili	10,5	1.050	1,146
Nigeria	77,0	380	865
Zaïre	16,2	140	457
Algeria	16,3	990	1,670
Marocco	17,2	540	1,230
	1.749,2		

Source: FAO, Trade Yearbook, 1976
         World Bank Atlas, 1977

(1) − = net exporter of cereals

n.a. = not available

ANNEX 3

Food and the New International Economic Order

Programme of Action on the Establishment of a New International Economic Order

The General Assembly
Adopts the following Programme of Action:

PROGRAMME OF ACTION ON THE ESTABLISHMENT OF A NEW INTERNATIO-
NAL ECONOMIC ORDER

In view of the continuing severe economic imbalance in the
relations between developed and developing countries, and in
the context of the constant and continuing aggravation of the
imbalance of the economies of the developing countries and the
consequent need for the mitigation of their current economic
difficulties, urgent and effective measures need to be taken
by the international community to assist the developing countries, while devoting particular attention to the least developed, landlocked and island countries and those developing
countries most seriously affected by economic crises and natural calamities leading to serious retardation of development
processes.

With a view to ensuring the application of the Declaration on
the Establishment of a New International Economic Order it
will be necessary to adopt and implement within a specified
period a programme of action of unprecedented scope and to
bring about maximum economic co-operation and understanding
among all States, particularly between developed and developing countries based on the principles of dignity and sovereign
equality.

Programme of Action on Food Problems

Food

All efforts should be made:
1. To take full account of specific problems of developing
   countries, particularly in times of food shortages, in the
   international efforts connected with the food problem.
2. To take into account that, owing to lack of means, some
   developing countries have vast potentialities of unexploit-
   ed of underexploited land which, if reclaimed and put into
   practical use, would contribute considerably to the solution of the food crisis.
3. By the international community to undertake concrete and
   speedy measures with a view to arresting desertification,
   salination, and damage by locusts or any other similar phenomenon involving several developing countries, particularly in Africa, and gravely affecting the capacity of agricultural production of these countries. Furthermore, the
   international community should assist the developing count-

ries affected by this phenomenon to develop the affected zones with a view to contributing to the solution of their food problems.

4. To refrain from damaging or deteriorating natural resources and food resources, especially those derived from the sea, by preventing pollution and taking appropriate steps to protect and reconstitute those resources.

5. By developed countries in evolving their policies relating to production, stocks, imports and exports of food to take full account of the interests of:
   - developing importing countries which cannot afford high prices for their imports, and
   - developing exporting countries which need increased market opportunities for their exports.

6. To ensure that developing countries can import the necessary quantity of food without undue strain on their foreign exchange resources and without unpredictable deterioration in their balance of payments. In this context, special measures should be taken in respect of the least developed, the land-locked and island developing countries as well as those developing countries most seriously affected by economic crises and natural calamities.

7. To ensure that concrete measures to increase food production and storage facilities in developing countries should be introduced, inter alia, by ensuring an increase in all available essential inputs, including fertilizers, from developed countries on favourable terms.

8. To promote exports of food production of developing countries through just and equitable arrangements, inter alia, by the progressive elimination of such protective and other measures as constitute unfair competition.

7 PRIMARY COMMODITIES AND THE NEW INTERNATIONAL ECONOMIC ORDER
Wouter Tims

7.1. INTRODUCTION

It is hardly necessary to repeat here the findings of an extensive literature on the trade of developing countries in primary commodities. Their trade has grown slowly, prices and earnings have been unstable, their processing hampered. What applied fifty years ago to these markets still applies in large measure today. Nor are the proposals to deal with the problems posed by these markets of only recent vintage. None less than J.M. Keynes proposed a "General Council for Commodity Controls", as he wrote (1) in 1942:

"The essence of the plan should be that prices are subject to gradual changes but are fixed within a reasonable range over short periods; those producers who find the ruling price attractive being allowed a gradual expansion at the expense of those who find it unattractive. Thus we should aim at combining a short-period stabilization of prices with a long-period price policy which balances supply and demand and allows a steady rate of expansion to the cheaper-cost producers."

The Keynes proposal was not adopted and several more recent proposals have met the same fate. The proposal of an Integrated Program for Commodities and a Common Fund, which in several respects resembles what Keynes advocated thirty years ago, is now going through a process of protracted negotiations - if the deliberations in UNCTAD can be so named - with meager chances of becoming reality. Notwithstanding the failure to achieve an international consensus on policies for primary commodities, the trade in them has grown over time. In leaps and bounds, no doubt, and with retrogressive characteristics when compared to other indicators of global economic development.

The present international discussion concerns, as it has for so many years, both the level of prices for primary commodities in international trade, and the stabilization of

131

prices. In addition, security of supply has resurfaced as a major issue, which is linked to the issue of national control over the production of primary commodities and over invest- ments related to their production and processing. In order to gauge the importance of these issues, a framework is needed describing the role of primary commodities in world trade and their significance for developing countries. This will be dealt with first, before discussing present policy proposals or possible alternatives.

7.2. MAIN FEATURES OF PRIMARY COMMODITY TRADE

The issues concerning international trade in primary commodi- ties are of particular concern to the developing countries; they depend for a large part of their export earnings on these commodities, which are mainly exported to the indus- trial countries. Primary commodities are a heterogeneous group (2) consisting of food and beverages, non-food agricul- tural products, fuels and other (non-fuel) minerals and me- tals. Also, they originate from different countries and have each their own particular destination patterns. Overall trends should therefore be looked at with some caution as those hide a variety of developments by countries and by groups of commodities. With that in mind, several general statements about primary commodities can be made at the start (and the basic statistics behind those are annexed):

1. The share of primary commodities excluding fuels (particu- larly oil) in world trade has declined; this trend is clearly borne out by the statistics over the years since World War II, which show a drop in that share from 47 per- cent around 1955 to 27 percent in 1975. As exports of the developing countries around 1950 consisted of more than 90 percent of primary commodities, it wil be clear that de- veloping countries were bound to see their share of world trade considerably reduced.
2. Within the (relatively) shrinking market for primary com- modities, the share of the developing countries has decli- ned significantly; around 1955 they supplied about 40 per- cent of the world's internationally-traded primary commo- dities, but in 1975 that share had fallen to only 28 per- cent.
3. Not all developing countries have suffered from these trends in equal measure, partly because of the wide diffe- rences in the composition of the commodities each exports and partly because of changing market shares among the de- veloping countries.

The causes of these developments are several and constitute a complex pattern. The first characteristic - the relative de- cline in importance of primary commodities in world trade - is usually linked to low income elasticities in the consuming countries. For some commodities, like coffee or cocoa, a high level of per capita consumption has been reached and it is

unlikely that consumption will rise much further when incomes
increase. Others are used as raw materials in industries
which in fact face similar market situations for their end-
products. No doubt the growth of demand as compared to income
growth in the consuming countries is an important factor;
available indices suggest however that world trade in primary
commodities (excluding fuels) in fact has kept pace with income growth, or has even exceeded it somewhat when measured
over the period 1955-1975. Although one ought to be cautious
with such statements, given the weak statistical basis of the
price and volume indices of world trade, it still seems unlikely that, on average, a low income elasticity played a role.
For some commodities slow demand growth undoubtedly did limit
the growth of trade, but for others the opposite probably
held.

The relative decline of primary commodities in world trade
also reflects another development quite unrelated to their
performance: trade in manufactured goods increased enormously
over the same period under the impetus of progressive trade
liberalization and economic integration by the industrial
countries. This process boosted the level and growth rate of
world trade, but it is unlikely that these factors will continue to operate as much in the future as they did in the
past. The relative decline of primary commodities in world
trade may therefore become less pronounced in the future.

A third reason suggested for the decline is the expansion
in the area of synthetic substitutes, which have intruded into the markets for primary commodities. The examples of synthetic fibers, rubber and, more recently, fructose syrups
replacing sugar, are well-known. Effects can be expected not
only on the volume of primary products trade, but also on the
prices of the latter, both presumably having to adjust downward. As to the volume effect, one would infer therefore that
demand for primary commodities could have increased by more
than the - still respectable - rate by which in fact it did
increase. As to prices, one enters at this point the area of
the long debate on the terms of trade of primary products
versus manufactured goods. That issue is at the root of much
discussion and negotiations concerning the developing countries' trade, and will therefore be dealt with more fully in
what follows, at a later point.

Considerably more worrisome is the decline of the share in
total trade in primary commodities supplied by exports from
developing countries. Again here, a number of hypotheses have
been stated that are meant to explain the erosion of the position of the developing countries, which accounted for about
half of the (non-fuel) total trade in primary commodities by
the end of the Second World War but barely more than a quarter of such trade in the most recent years.

Firstly, commodity composition can hardly be blamed. World
trade in primary commodities increased on average (in value
terms) by 8.1 percent per annum, and if exports of developing
countries by broad commodity groups in the base year 1955 had
shown the same growth rates as apply to these groups in world

trade, then their exports would have increased by 7.8 percent
per annum. Although this suggests a slightly unfavorable composition it is a long way from explaining why exports of primary commodities from developing countries increased over
that period by only 6.1 percent per annum in value terms.

Declining shares in trade did not occur in all commodity
groups. A one-third share was maintained in trade of ores and
crude minerals, and a slightly smaller share applied to nonferrous metals over the period. (3) The declines are concentrated in the other two categories: food, beverages, oils and
fats, and agricultural raw materials. Within those, clearly
some stand out as below-average performers, notably the beverage crops - coffee, tea and cocoa - and the cereals amongst
the food group, and the oil seeds and fibers amongst the raw
materials of agricultural origin. Also rubber shows only me-
diocre performance in this category.

The beverage crops are almost exclusively produced and exported by developing countries. Their slow growth can partly
be attributed to saturation of traditional markets and competition from locally-produced soft drinks in potential new
markets. As a consequence, volume growth in beverages over
the past twenty years amounted to a meager 1.8 percent per
year of exports, and prices tended to fall in the long run.
The weak performance of these commodities accounts for a significant part of the declining share in the food category.

Cereals are exported by only a small number of developing
countries, notably Argentina (wheat), Thailand and Burma
(rice). In volume terms, both have been far from buoyant:
wheat export volumes increased by about 3.5 percent per year,
but the trend in rice exports was slightly downward. Most developing countries have experienced the need to import food
grains, some in increasing quantities. Exports have thus
been hampered by the slow growth of domestic food supplies,
particularly in the most populous and poorest developing
countries.

The fibers - cotton, jute and wool particularly - have
been exposed to the competition of synthetic substitutes. Although this does explain a modest rate of growth of exports,
it does not explain why, for example, cotton from developing
countries experienced a reduction of its share in the world
cotton market. The volume of developing countries' exports
actually declined somewhat over time, whereas world trade
maintained a modest expansion, mainly originating in cen-
trally-planned economies, i.c. the Soviet Union. Domestic
supply constraints have therefore undoubtedly played a role,
as textile industries in the developing countries claimed a
rising share of cotton output, thus reducing export availabi-
lities. To some extent, cotton exports have been replaced by
exports of textiles (yarns and cloth) and of ready-made
clothing.

Oil seeds mostly showed trendwise volume declines, but
soybeans are an exception. Also, one should note the rapid
growth of vegetable oil exports which are extracted from
these seeds. Similarly oil meals and cakes showed considerable expansion, which points to the fact that local processing

for export has made progress in this commodity category.

Summing up, one finds a broad range of developments on both the demand and supply sides which have caused the unsatisfactory performance of primary commodity exports of the developing countries. In several instances it appears that the loss of market shares is not the consequence of losses per individual commodity, but more the result of a different composition within each broad product category. In others, losses are compensated by expanded exports of processed products. And the cases in which one can point to slow growth of demand - sometimes under the influence of synthetics competition - are matched by other cases in which supply constraints hampered the growth of international trade.

No doubt other factors applied as well. One commonly stated factor is the reduced security of supply - whether real or perceived - after the process of decolonization and, sometimes, nationalization of production facilities. The argument that quality and timeliness could no longer be trusted to be maintained runs mostly along the same lines. Such perceptions are hard to quantify, let alone to be proven true or false. It would be overly confident to entirely reject the argument, but in the absence of representative information one should not put too much weight on it.

Not all developing countries fared the same in their exports of primary products. Some rely on one or two commodities only for almost their entire export earnings, whereas others have more diversified primary commodity exports, or increasingly export manufactured goods. Countries which, before 1960, depended more than 90, percent on exports of primary commodities, experienced a median growth of exports through the mid-seventies of 4.5 percent per year, but the countries which started out with more diversified exports in the beginning experienced a median growth rate (in volume terms) of about 7 percent. Among the large group of countries depending almost exclusively on primary commodities, a further distinction can be made by their level of poverty. It appears that the poorest (and most populous) countries with 1975 per capita incomes of $ 250 or less experienced a median export growth rate of only 3.4 percent per annum, compared to the 5.1 percent rate observed for the more advanced developing countries. Given those trends of the past, it is an ominous sign that virtually all of the poorest countries which depended almost exclusively on primary commodities in 1960, still do so in 1976.

7.3. PRICES, STABILITY AND THE TERMS OF TRADE

The market conditions which were faced by primary commodities and more in particular the tropical agricultural products, were clearly of a kind which induced a weak price trend. Slow growth of demand and the competition from synthetics could easily lead to excess supplies, even if supplies from the developing countries were not increasing all that much. Policies in the EEC which provided incentives to production with-

in that region and protected the market against imports - as
for example in the case of sugar -- had the same effect and
tended to depress prices in the open international markets.

How badly the developing countries fared as a consequence
remains a matter of contention: one should compare the price
performance of primary commodities to some yardstick of international prices before conclusions can be reached. A number of
such comparisons is possible and the results are clearly different from one to the other. For example, one comparison
measures a price index of primary commodities in international trade against a price index of traded manufactured goods.
The thought behind this is that developing countries export
mainly primary commodities and use their export earnings to
import manufactured goods. Thus, the price ratio development
over time should tell us something about the international
purchasing power of primary goods exporters. As this ratio has
gradually declined, by about 1.5 percent on average per year
between 1953 and 1976, the conclusion would be that international price developments have annually reduced the purchasing
power of primary goods exporters by that percentage.

One should, however, take account of two developments
which took place with respect to the composition of trade of
the developing countries. Over time, the dependence on primary
commodities as their mainstay of exports declined; also their
imports of primary commodities increased substantially, particularly if oil is included in this total. In 1975 primary
commodities excluding oil accounted for about a quarter of
total imports of the developing countries, and for 40 percent
when oil is added. These shares have shown fluctuations over
time, but have in the long run been fairly stable; the value
of primary commodity imports rose at about the same rate as
total imports by an average of 11 percent per year since 1955
in value terms. With respect to their exports, non-primary
exports as a share of total non-oil exports rose from 10 percent in 1955 to 43 percent in 1975. It should be noted that
these totals and averages for the developing countries as a
group hide considerable intercounty differences, but for an
understanding of the terms of trade issue, the totals are to
be looked at first, before an analysis of trends by subgroups
of developing countries.

The worsening of the price ratio between primary commodities and manufactured goods is, in many cases, not a good indicator of the income losses to which the developing countries
as a group were exposed. But one is also hard put to come up
with a good indicator of what in fact happened. If one includes the oil-exporting developing countries in the group,
one finds that the terms of trade for the developing countries have improved immensely since 1973, but this does no
justice to the fact that only a few of the countries benefit-
ted from the oil price increase whereas most suffered. Similarly, exports of manufactures cushioned the terms of trade of
some countries, but for many others this did not apply. It is
clear, therefore, that the terms-of-trade issue requires a
suitable classification by subgroups of countries if the analysis is to be useful.

Excluding the major oil exporting countries and thus looking separately at the larger country group which consists
mainly of the oil-importers, one is faced with serious problems of interpreting the evidence. Firstly, one cannot take
the mid-fifties as the basis because of the relatively high
commodity prices prevailing after the Korean war. But over
the shorter period, from 1960, it is not clear whether a trend
applies to the terms of trade of these developing countries.
IMF data suggest a gradual improvement between 1960 and the
early seventies, followed by a sharp deterioration as a consequence of the oil price increase and the recession in the
industrial countries. UNCTAD calculations - which appear to
have a better country coverage but sometimes use weak statistical materials - suggest fluctuations during the period
1960-1974, but no discernable upward or downward trend. The
latter is, however, a possibility if one is willing to extend
the data back to the mid-fifties.

Further breakdowns by country groups lead to the impression
that the lack of a trend during the sixties and early seventies is apparent in the terms of trade of the more advanced
developing countries with per capita incomes above $ 250 in
1975. If, for that group of countries, the mid-fifties are
taken as the base, a case can be made for a downward trend in
their terms of trade, possibly by up to half a percentage
point per year. The decline appears to be reduced over time,
which might be the result of the growing share of manufactured
goods in the exports of these countries.

The poorest countries, identified by per capita incomes of
$ 250 and less in 1975, did indeed, throughout both the short-
er and the longer period, experience terms of trade losses, at
a rate of roughly one percent per year. As these countries depend more heavily on primary commodities throughout the period,
this observation is not entirely unexpected. Thus it seems
that the terms of trade issue becomes, increasingly over time,
a problem of the poorest countries which have not as yet been
in a position to diversify their exports. It should, however,
be noted also that the distinction between country groups
purely on an income basis (which unfortunately is all that
published statistics supply) is not entirely satisfactory. One
finds exceptions to the stated conclusion on both sides of the
line: India and Pakistan, though poor, are significant exporters of manufactured goods, whereas Malaysia and Thailand did
not experience significant terms of trade losses although
their exports are almost exclusively composed of primary commodities.

The second issue concerning prices has to do with their instability over time. Sharp fluctuations have occurred in the past,
partly because of stock changes which accentuated price movements during cyclical peaks and troughs, partly also because
of low short-run supply elasticities of many primary commodities. For countries which depend on the earnings from primary
commodities to finance a major part of their imports, and frequently a significant part of domestic government expenditures,
this poses problems. Development programs may have to be curt-

ailed at times of low prices, whereas during periods of buoyant markets the danger of overcommitment to new expenditures
threatens the continuity of development programs.

In the past, efforts were made to deal with stabilization
of prices through international agreements which set a limited range for the price of a commodity and provided for buffer
stock operations and production or export quotas; more recently attempts have been made to obtain commitments from consuming countries to purchase minimum quantities. Attempts have
also been made to stabilize earnings of producing countries, by
individual commodities as under the EEC's Stabex program, or
for total export earnings as is provided for under Compensatory Finance from the International Monetary Fund. Agreements
exist only for a few commodities at present; the Stabex scheme
is limited both by commodities and by countries, whereas the
IMF's resources compensate only for part of earnings fluctuations. Stabilization   therefore remains an important issue.

Summing up the experience of the past twenty years, it would
appear that most countries depending heavily on exports of
primary commodities have been exposed to considerable risks.
Growth of the demand for some of these products has been slow
and substitution by synthetics has made inroads into their
markets. Still, for many of the small and poor nations the
chances for export diversification are remote. Prices of primary commodities have been volatile and the terms of trade of
the developing countries have at best remained stable, whereas for some of the most vulnerable countries they declined.
For all of those reasons the issue of international policies
which promise improvements for primary goods exporters have
been high on the agenda for many years.

To these issues one was added more recently in the wake of
the OPEC action on oil, which also raised the specter of supply limitations for essential commodities which could disrupt
the economies of the industrial countries. Security of supply
has therefore become an item on the agenda; it is clear that
arrangements on this point are important for the developing
countries as well, for example, with respect to food grains
for which many of these countries depend on international
market supplies.

7.4. POLICY PROPOSALS AND NEGOTIATIONS

The agreements reached in the past for individual commodities
or groups of countries and commodities have only removed part
of the problems concerning primary commodity trade. A new impetus was given to international negotiations at the time of
the OPEC action of 1973, coinciding with extremely high international prices for many primary commodities. It seemed, at
least for a while, that the unilateral regulation of supply
and prices by producers would become the new and promising
avenue for primary commodity exporters to obtain better and
more stable prices for their products. At the same time the
perceived threat of supply curtailment and more unilaterally
imposed price increases were incentives to the consuming

- mainly industrial countries - to participate in new negotiations for the regulation of international primary commodity markets. Under the aegis of the New International Economic Order, several new proposals were tabled and submitted for negotiation.

This New Order should not be understood in terms of a fully designed blueprint of changed international relations. No doubt, in the special sessions of the U.N. General Assembly dealing with the New International Economic Order, a number of principles were laid down which should be at the basis of these relationships. But the specific proposals made as part of its action program can hardly be considered adequate to bring these principles to life. The proposals deal largely with issues that had been on the agenda for much longer, like price stabilization, measures to relieve the debt burden, and control over natural resources. However, the new proposals could claim to be both more general and bolder, and in some respects to add some new elements.

In the field of primary commodities, such a new element was the specific form of the demand by the developing countries to make international agreements which would raise prices of primary commodities. Remunerative prices had been on the agenda since the early sixties, but the proposal to attempt an indexation of those prices went further in some respects than earlier suggestions regarding price levels. The rationale for proposals of this kind was not only the perception that prices of primary commodities had in fact lagged behind those of internationally-traded manufactures, but also the belief that the power of OPEC to raise the oil price unilaterally was to some extent transferable to other commodities. No doubt, the global studies which predicted serious scarcities of several key commodities in the future strengthened the belief of both producers and consumers in the possibilities of sharp long-term price rises for those commodities. In itself, this contributed to the willingness of the industrial countries to negotiate.

For a time, the negotiations took place on two fronts, in UNCTAD as well as in the Committee for International Economic Cooperation (CIEC), the latter's efforts better known as the North-South dialogue. The UNCTAD forum was of course the most logical, and specific proposals for a comprehensive set of policies concerning primary commodity trade had been prepared by its staff. The CIEC was seen by the industrial countries as a body which would deal exclusively with the issues of pricing and supply security for oil. The developing countries did, however, insist that a much broader range of trade issues and problems of international finance be included in the dialogue. By the end of 1976 the North-South dialogue came to its end with a declaration rich in words but poor in meaningful decisions; for some time there had been a virtual stalemate on most major issues. From then on, the locus of the negotiations shifted fully to UNCTAD.

The centerpiece of the discussions in Geneva has now, for a number of years, been the Integrated Program for Commodities and the proposal for a Common Fund to finance operations in commodity markets. The objectives are again to obtain remune-

rative prices and to achieve a greater measure of stability
in commodity markets. But instead of attempting arrangements
by individual commodities, the proposal suggested combining
arrangements for a substantial number of commodities. To some
extent this was to attain a higher efficiency in the use of
financial resources needed for buffer stock operations: it is
unlikely that price fluctuations will be simultaneous for all
commodities, so that finances accruing to the buffer stock
authority from sales in the market of one commodity can be
applied to the procurement of stocks in other commodity markets if prices approach the lower bound of the agreed price
range.

A more important reason for an integrated approach stemmed
from the experience of the past in negotiating arrangements
for individual commodities. When market prices are high and
rising, consuming countries tend to be in favour of stabilization   agreements as those can shave the price peaks. But
producing countries are much less inclined at that point in
time to negotiate. In a situation of declining and low prices, the situation around the negotiating table tends to re-
verse itself. No doubt this has been one reason for the difficulties in the past in achieving agreements on market stabilization.

An integrated approach has major advantages in this respect, particularly if one brings together a group of commodities with different sets of consuming and producing countries.
Each country will then find itself in a position of being a
consumer of some and a producer of others. His lack of interest in some commodities because of actual prices in the international market being in a country's favour will be balanced by strong interest in others where prevailing prices do
hurt this country's economy. It is then possible to push a
large package of commodity arrangements through, as every
participating country will be able to point to some immediate
benefits which are expected to at least balance the costs.

During the UNCTAD negotiations the proposal was gradually
made less attractive by changing and reducing the commodity
coverage. Probably the worst blow was the decision to negotiate again by individual commodities and to postpone their
integration to a later stage. But even before that happened
there had been other threats to the proposal which were of
a more fundamental nature; what actually happened in the course of the negotiations can easily be interpreted as a skill-
ful tactic by the major opponents of the proposal to side-
track the deliberations and to reduce the chances of success.
These fundamental objections came from some of the industrial
countries (notably Germany and Japan) and raised the question
of whether it could really be to the common good if arrangements were made that would tamper with the groundrules of
free trade. From that viewpoint it might not be at all desirable to try to stabilize prices; but of course the concept of
remunerative prices could find even less favour in that light.

It need hardly be said that this position is a hypocritical
one. Within developed countries the stabilization of agricultural prices has been accepted practice for a long time, and
the explicit linkage of the price levels of agricultural prod-

ucts to the objective of maintaining and improving levels of
farm incomes constitutes a clear case of setting remunerative
prices. Although systems of price determination and price and
income support differ from country to country and over time,
this has been a rather common feature of economic policies in
developed countries. It is therefore difficult to accept the
position taken on international price stabilization and higher prices in international trade.

This policy contradiction becomes even more rejectable
when account is taken of the effects which domestic price and
incomes policies for agriculture have had on international
trade and prices, particularly for developing countries producing competing agricultural products. Changes in the market
and price situation for sugar provide a good example. The
comparative advantages of cane sugar over beet sugar have been
established reasonably clearly, but policies in the EEC and,
untill 1974, in the USA, favoured domestic producers and maintained or increased the degree of self-sufficiency in those
markets at the expense of imports. This reduced the free international market for sugar to a small residual market characterized by large price fluctuations. For periods of several
years at a time it reduced prices to levels at which efficient
producers among the developing countries were unable to provide for adequate maintenance of existing sugar mills, even
less to invest in new ones. With this in mind, a refusal to
cooperate for the purpose of stable and remunerative prices to
efficient producers by some of those who were instrumental in
destabilizing the international market can only be condemned.

The free trade argument could only reasonably be defended
if there were free trade indeed. But in fact that situation
does not at all prevail. A study made by the World Bank in
1975 (4) suggested that imports of nine selected primary commodities by the OECD countries would be 38 percent larger in
1980 with full liberalization as compared to a continuation of
present policies; about three-fourths, equivalent to $ 7 bil-
lion in 1974 prices, would originate in the developing countries, or 8 percent above the level of total primary exports
than was to be expected under unchanged policies. It is highly
improbable that a liberalization will come to pass, as it
would require the dismantling of the EEC's common agricultural
policy. But against that background it seems even more reasonable to expect the industrial countries to agree to a comparatively modest proposal like the Integrated Program for Commodities, and to provide a good part of the needed financial
resources.

The proposal has some characteristics which should not be
left unnoted as they relate to the position of a number of
very poor and relatively small countries which earlier were
identified as the weakest partners in international trade.
Those countries have only a small share in total exports of
the developing countries, not more than about 15 percent in
recent years. It is therefore to be expected that the bulk of
the benefits of stabilization will accrue to the more advanced developing countries (the same applies to liberalization as
well), whereas the countries most in need will only be helped
marginally. For the latter group it applies more generally

that their development problems can only be relieved to a limited extent through policies related to their trade.

The duration and present state of negotiations around the Integrated Program suggests that some limited results may in the end be achieved, but to expect more would be overly optimistic. This leaves for the time being the Stabex scheme of the EEC and the IMF's compensatory finance facility. The first has flaws as it is limited to specific commodities and countries and uses a compensation formula which does not take account of the general price increases in world trade. The negotiations for its next stage as part of Lomé II have just begun and may lead to improvements. The IMF has, over the years, improved the access to compensatory finance in several ways and has become a major and flexible resource for developing countries experiencing export short-falls. But this financing takes the form of medium-term loans at a low interest rate, and increases indebtedness.

7.5. COMMODITY TRADE POLICIES AND THE CHANGING DEVELOPMENT PRIORITIES

The development experience of the past twenty-five years demonstrated the capacity of developing countries to achieve rapid growth, but also the inequity of its distribution. Between countries the gaps tended to widen as the poorest countries had the lowest rates of economic growth; within countries the benefits of growth accrued to a small part of the population, whereas the poorest groups remained in the same situation and saw their total numbers swell further. The search is on, therefore, for policies and programs which can deal with the distributional issues, both between and within countries.

It is therefore important to extend the discussion of policy proposals in the field of primary commodity trade somewhat further and to raise the issue of their distributive impact, both between and within countries. On that point there is only little discussion in the literature; one could, with some justification, conclude that two separate dialogues exist, of which one concerns the distributive development problems and the other a set of measures concerning trade and capital flows, with only few links between the two, particularly with respect to trade measures.

A first question must therefore be: to what extent can different groups of developing countries be expected to benefit from a stabilization program along the lines of the UNCTAD proposal for an integrated program? For demonstration purposes in addressing this question, ten commodities have been grouped below which, at one time or another, have ranked high on the list for inclusion in the scheme: cocoa, coffee, tea, sugar, jute, cotton, sisal, rubber, copper and tin. Some of the market characteristics of these commodities are summarized in Table 1.

Table 1
Market characteristics of selected commodities

	cocoa	coffee	tea	sugar	jute	cotton	sisal	rubber	copper	tin
1) LDC share in world production (%)	100.0	98.7	65.5	40.8	72.9	36.8	n.a.	98.3	39.5	73.6
2) LDC share in world exports (%)	100.0	95.6	82.1	52.5	97.5	46.1	97.7	99.4	59.5	80.9
3) LDC share in world imports (%)	2.1	5.5	31.2	24.6	38.2	27.0	n.a.	10.0	5.0	12.4
4) Low Income countries (≤ $ 250):										
a) share in LDC-exports of the commodity (%)	4.7	20.7	94.6	3.4	79.1	32.4	40.5	30.6	20.2	14.1
b) share of the commodity in country-group exports (%)	0.4	6.1	5.6	0.7	1.7	5.4	0.3	3.0	5.1	0.9

Sources: IBRD, Commodity Trade and Price Trends (1975 edition), for lines 3a and 3b (average 1970–1972); Price Prospects for Major Primary Commodities, June 1978, for lines 1 and 2.

It should be noted that these ten commodities are characterized by mostly very large shares of developing countries in
their international trade; only for cotton is the share less
than 50 percent, for sugar and copper between 50 and 60 percent. Shares of world production are usually somewhat less,
except for coffee. As a crude measure of distribution, line 4)
shows the part which developing countries with per capita incomes of $ 250 or less in 1976 took in exports of each of the
commodities by all developing countries together; except for
tea and jute, these shares are mostly less than 40 percent and,
for the ten commodities together, account for about 23 percent
in 1975. As the last row indicates, the share of these commodities in total exports of the low income group of countries
amount to 5-6 percent for coffee, tea, cotton and copper. The
aggregate share of the ten commodities in their total exports
is 29 percent in 1975.

It appears that the ten commodities choosen here would benefit the low income countries slightly more than average, as
these countries account for 16 percent of total developing
countries' exports whereas their share in the ten commodities
is higher, at 23 percent. But this marginal advantage is far
from sufficient to compensate for (a) the lesser participation of low income countries in international trade, (5) (b)
their lower income and greater need, and (c) their larger population.

Suppose that it was intended to raise incomes per capita
in all developing countries by the same absolute amount (and
thus by a much larger percentage in the low income countries
compared to the others). Given the population in each of the
two income groups, this would require $ 1.40 to be spent in
the low income countries for each $ 1.00 spent in the other
group of countries, or a share of close to 60 percent for the
low income countries in total expenditures, which is 2½ times
the share they can expect to get under the commodity arrangement designed above. In fact, a 23 percent share in the expected benefits is only marginally better than a proposal to
raise incomes in all developing countries by the same percentage. Given the gap between the per capita incomes of the two
country groups ($ 160 versus $ 1,020 in 1976) this appears
inappropriate for distributive reasons.

These calculations do not take account of the particular
demand, supply and price elasticities pertaining to the ten
commodities, but their performance in the past suggests that
the commodities most inportant for the low income countries
are the ones with the least favourable market outlook (particularly tea and jute). Therefore it may be doubted whether
the market share of the low income countries, presently at
23 percent, is an appropriate indicator for the share these
countries can expect out of the total benefits. In fact, the
present trade share may be considered a maximum for the share
of the benefits.

The exposition given here does not purport to say that international measures to stabilize and increase prices of primary commodities are in themselves less desirable policies.
It only suggests that such trade measures are, however, not

easily brought in line with the objective of channeling resources preferentially to low income countries. In other
words: trade policies of the type suggested and discussed
are a poor substitute for aid policies, as the former cannot
but the latter can, be directed to countries and regions considered to be of high priority in development cooperation.

Finally the effects of international commodity arrangements
on domestic income distribution in commodity producing countries need to be discussed. Clearly, one enters an area here
which could stand a lot more data collection and analysis;
little is known for sure and the few things about which data
exist may bias one's perceptions on the basis of inadequate
evidence. One should therefore limit the discussion to a survey of relevant issues, with illustrations for particular
commodities, countries and time periods.
    The distribution of income generated by the production and
export of primary commodities will depend on the organization
of production and on the policies of the government in the
producing country. Of more interest is the question, however,
as to what happens when (national and/or international) prices fluctuate. And in close relation to that question, one
needs to know who benefits from price stabilization, in terms
of distributive shares. In the latter analysis one cannot limit the scope to the effects in producing countries; as the
data in Table 1 show (line 3), for some commodities the developing countries are also major importers. And in addition
to the ten commodities listed there, one needs to include
food grains, for which separate measures are being negotiated at present which are of paramount importance for the food-
deficit developing countries.

The organization of production, and the policies of governments toward the producers of primary commodities vary widely. In some cases, governments own the production facilities
themselves, as is the case for copper. The consequences of
price fluctuations are in that case largely borne by the
government budget; as in most countries the workers in minerals production are relatively better organized and wield
political influence, their wages tend to be more rigid than
those of other lower income groups. In times of high international prices the government may not be able to resist the
pressure to increase wages - skewing the income distribution - whereas in times of low prices the government may only
be in a position to lower their real income by inflationary
financing of its budget deficit. Inflation tends to reduce
the purchasing power of lower income groups more than other
(mainly non-wage) incomes.
    For several agricultural export crops, it applies that a
major part of output originates on estates or plantations, a
growing portion of which have been brought under public control through nationalization. This is the case for example
for most Asian tea production, parts of rubber production
(Indonesia, West Africa) and, in some cases, cocoa production.
In addition, in many producing countries there are arrangements for the procurement of these crops on behalf of the

government at regulated prices which normally are below the equivalent of the prevailing international price. In other cases governments may refrain from direct involvement in domestic trade but levy export taxes which may vary with international price movements an/or take account of safeguarding adequate supplies at reasonable prices for the domestic market.

Fluctuations in international prices therefore do not in all cases reach the producer, as he may be shielded from price movements by the government's price policy. This has the advantage that supply fluctuations are reduced and an expansion of production can take place gradually over time - rather than in leaps and bounds - as long as the regulated price is kept at a level which producers find adequate to keep producing and investing in that crop. It has the disadvantage that price increases which reflect real supply shortages in the international market do not lead to an adequate increase of the supply.

To the extent that more stable prices lead to an improved income stream for private estates and plantations, the effects on income distribution depend on the strength of trade unions and government to make the owners pass on part of the gains to the labour force. The general situation in the labour market will no doubt also influence the degree to which a redistribution is to take place. For smaller farmers the same may apply to a lesser extent, although they are already in most countries, shielded from gains or losses by government price policies.

It appears therefore that one of the main beneficiaries of more stable, and particularly of more remunerative, prices will be the government of the producing and exporting country, through larger fiscal revenues from export levies and taxes or increased profits of its marketing boards. The effects on the income distribution will depend on whether and how the government intends to spend these additional resources, accruing in the form of foreign exchange. This raises in turn the question of general government policies and the degree to which distributive objectives form part of their design.

Without attempting an exhaustive survey along those lines, it can nevertheless be said that strong distributive policies effectively implemented by the authorities, are still rare in the developing world, although most development plans and policy pronouncements would suggest a better situation. Under these circumstances it seems rather unlikely that improvements in the price performance of primary commodity markets would result in improvements of the income distribution in the producing countries. No doubt in some cases, like that of smallholder rubber producers in Thailand and Indonesia, or that of tea-growers in East Africa under outgrower's schemes, the beneficiaries may belong to the lower strata of the income distribution, but particularly when governments themselves can channel a major part of additional income to their own revenues, greater equity seems an unlikely result. The same applies for developing countries importing primary com-

modities (food grains in particular) as governments usually
monopolize the import trade and will be the first to benefit
from more stable prices. It then depends on the direction of
its additional expenditures, whether equity is improved.

7.6. CONCLUDING REMARKS

Summing up, it appears that discussions of international policy measures concerning primary commodities should
take account, to a larger extent than presently is the case,
of the national policies which are their complements. One
cannot close one's eyes to the latter if one professes, at
other points of the development debate, to be concerned about
the poorest countries and population groups within those
countries.

Table 2

Main indicators of trade in primary commodities

	1955	1960	1965	1970	1975
World Exports (value, mln. $)	93,540	127,870	186,390	312,070	872,220
Of which: Primary commodities excluding fuels (% share)	39,480 (47.4)	48,200 (41.8)	62,450 (37.1)	86,670 (30.6)	187,690 (26.7)
Fuels, energy	10,270 (11.0)	12,640 (9.9)	17,920 (9.6)	28,670 (9.2)	169,130 (19.4)
Exports from Developing Countries (value, mln. $)	23,730	27,390	36,490	54,980	210,480
Of which: fuels other exports	5,900 17,830	7,650 19,740	11,310 25,180	18,100 36,880	125,170 85,310
LDC exports of primary commodities, excl. fuels	15,910	17,100	20,470	26,900	52,300
Share of LDC's in world trade (%) excl. fuels	(21.4)	(17.1)	(15.0)	(13.0)	(12.1)
Share of LDC's in non-fuels primary commodity trade (%)	(40.3)	(35.5)	(32.8)	(31.0)	(27.9)
World trade in non-fuels primary commodities: Food, beverages, oils and fats Agricultural raw materials Ores and crude minerals Non-ferrous metals	 20,430 12,030 3,420 3,600	 24,810 13,820 5,000 4,570	 34,340 15,080 6,340 6,690	 45,830 18,140 10,490 12,210	 115,030 34,010 20,590 18,060
total	39,480	48,200	62,450	86,670	187,690
LDC exports of non-fuels primary commodities: Food, beverages, oils and fats Agricultural raw materials Ores and crude minerals Non-ferrous metals	 8,700 4,860 1,130 1,220	 9,210 5,000 1,540 1,350	 11,680 4,730 2,150 1,910	 14,570 5,500 3,290 3,540	 33,090 8,650 6,610 3,950
total	15,910	17,100	20,470	26,900	52,300
LDC-share in world exports of: Food, beverages, oils and fats Agricultural raw materials Ores and crude minerals Non-ferrous metals	 42.8 40.4 33.0 33.9	 37.1 36.2 30.8 29.5	 34.0 31.4 33.9 28.6	 31.8 30.8 31.4 29.0	 28.8 25.4 32.1 21.9
total	40.3	35.5	32.8	31.0	27.9

Source: UNCTAD Handbook 1976, Annex Tables; UN Monthly Bull. of Stat. June 1978,
Spec. Table F. Fuels, SITC 3; food, SITC 0 + 1 + 22 + 4; agric. raw mat.,
SITC 2 - (22 + 27 + 28); ores, SITC 27 + 28, nonf. met., SITC 68.

FOOTNOTES

1. In a paper he wrote in April 1942 in the U.K. Treasury as part of the preparations for the Bretton Woods Conference. I am grateful to Mr. L. Jayawardena for bringing these papers to my attention.

2. Unless otherwise stated, references to primary commodities will be to those in categories 0-4 and division 68 of the Standard International Trade Classification (SITC, Rev.).

3. The low share in 1975 is not representative as considerable de-stocking took place at low prices in international markets.

4. Bank Staff Working Paper no. 193: Possible Effects of Trade Liberalization on Trade in Primary Commodities, Washington DC, January 1975.

5. Exports as a percent of GNP in 1975 were about 10% for low income countries and 18% for other developing countries (excluding major oil exporters).

REFERENCES[*]

Adams, F. Gerald and Sonia A. Klein (editors): Stabilizing World Commodity Markets, Lexington/Toronto, 1978. Probably the best current survey of the relevant literature.

IBRD/IMF, Stabilization of Prices of Primary Commodities (in 3 parts), Washington DC, 1969.

Brook, E.M. and E.R. Grilli: "Commodity Price Stabilization and the Developing World", in Finance and Development 14, 1 (March): 8-11.

Commodity Trade and Price Trends, (EC-166) issues of the years 1971 through 1978, Commodities and Export Projections Division, World Bank, Washington DC.

IBRD Working Paper no. 245, Stabilization, Adjustment and Diversification: A Study of the Weakest Commodities Produced by the Poorest Regions, Nov. 1976, Washington DC.

IBRD Working Paper no. 193, Possible Effects of Trade Liberalization on Trade in Primary Commodities, Jan. 1975, Washington DC.

UNCTAD, An Integrated Commodity Programme, Geneva 1976.

[*]Out of the vast literature on primary commodities, only the main sources used are mentioned here.

8 THE NORTH-SOUTH DIALOGUE: ANOTHER CONFRONTATION OR A BASIS FOR A NEW INTERNATIONAL ECONOMIC ORDER?

Edmund P. Wellenstein

8.1. INTRODUCTORY REMARKS

Since this paper will appear more than a year after the final
ministerial session of the Conference on International Economic Cooperation (officially CIEC; it became, however, generally known as the 'North-South Dialogue') which took place in
Paris between December 1975 and June 1977, it may be appropriate to recall in some detail the main features of that conference. Only against the background of the concrete function-
ing and of the results of the Paris dialogue is it possible to
assess whether this particular meeting has contributed further
to confrontational attitudes or to the establishment of a new
consensus between 'North' and 'South'. (2)
 CIEC introduced many innovations (in its shape and structure, its procedures, its methods of discussion, etc.) in the
field of international conference techniques. What distinguish-
ed CIEC from, in particular, those conferences on economic
North-South problems which take place under the aegis of the
United Nations may be summarized as follows:
1. the number of participants (members) which was limited as
 much as feasible, but was nevertheless as representative
 as possible of the different categories of countries (poor
 and rich, with or without oil, with or without raw materials, populous or thinly-populated, great or small, belonging to all five continents, etc.);
2. a work-programme in which the many different economic aspects of the North-South relation could come up for discussion both separately and in their interrelationship, in a
 matter-of-fact and concrete fashion, avoiding speeches 'to
 the gallery';
3. a strictly limited duration and as light as possible an infrastructure, that is, a purely administrative secretariat
 without any policy-functions;
4. a jointly-shared chairmanship, i.e., two 'co-chairmen',
 both for the conference itself and for the four permanent
 commissions, so that responsibility for the business in

150

hand proceeding apace was divided equally between exponents of the developing countries on the one hand and exponents of the industrial countries on the other;
5. decision-making by 'real' consensus, i.e. not an apparent meeting of minds which might in fact be enfeebled later by means of unilateral declarations, interpretations of 'sou-sentendus'.

As to participation in and organization of the CIEC we may refer in addition to paragraphs 5 to 9 (see below) of the Final Declaration of the ministerial meeting, which gave the official starting-signal for the conference in Paris in December 1975. As co-chairmen of the CIEC, the Venezuelan minister Perez Guerrero and the Canadian minister for Foreign Affairs, MacEachen, had been appointed in that capacity on this occasion.

The CIEC maintained a certain connection with the United Nations, the Secretary-General of which spoke at the two ministerial meetings and the Secretariat of which had a permanent observer in all commissions, in addition to the observers from the specialized international agencies inside and outside the United Nations family. Moreover the CIEC presented to the United Nations a report on the proceedings and results of the conference, which was submitted to the General Assembly in September 1977 (see below).

8.2. THE STRUCTURE OF CIEC

Excerpt from the Final Declaration of the Ministerial Session which took place from 16 till 19 December 1975, in Paris, and by which the CIEC was opened officially:
'5. The conference has decided to initiate an intensive international dialogue. For this purpose it has set up four commissions (for energy, raw materials, development and financial affairs) which will meet at periodic intervals throughout 1976. It has been agreed that each of the four commissions will consist of fifteen members, ten representing developing countries and five representing the industrialized states.
'6. The commissions will commence their activities on 11 February 1976. The preparation of the activities of the four commissions will be examined during a meeting of the co-chairmen of the conference and of the four commissions after due consultation of the other participants in the conference. This meeting will be held on 26 January 1976, in the context of the general debate referred to in paragraphs 10-14 of the Final Declaration of the second preparatory meeting, which were approved and ratified by the conference.
'7. The conference has agreed that the commissions will consist of the following participations:
- energy: Algeria, Saudi-Arabia, Brazil, Canada, EEC, Egypt, US, India, Iraq, Iran, Jamaica, Japan, Switzerland, Venezuela, Zaire;

- raw materials: Argentina, Australia, Cameroon, EEC, Spain, US, Indonesia, Japan, Mexico, Nigeria, Peru, Venezuela, Yugoslavia, Zaire, Zambia;
- development: Algeria, Argentina, Cameroon, Canada, EEC, US, India, Jamaica, Japan, Nigeria, Pakistan, Peru, Sweden, Yugoslavia, Zaire;
- finance: Saudi-Arabia, Brazil, EEC, Egypt, US, India, Indonesia, Iran, Japan, Mexico, Pakistan, Sweden, Switzerland, Zambia.

The co-chairmen of the commissions will be:
- energy: Saudi-Arabia and the US;
- raw materials: Japan and Peru;
- development: Algeria and EEC;
- finance: EEC and Iran.

If the need arises, joint meetings of the co-chairmen of the conference and the commissions will be convened.

'8. It has been agreed that members of the conference who would like to attend the work of a commission to which they do not belong are entitled to delegate a representative in the capacity of auditor without the right to speak to the meetings of this commission.

'9. The conference has decided that a specific number of functional intergovernmental organizations which are directly concerned with the relevant problems could make a useful contribution to its discussions. Therefore it has invited these organizations (Secretariat of the UN, OPEC, IEA, UNCTAD, OECD, FAO, GATT, UNDP, UNIDO, IBRD, IMF, SELA) to be represented on a permanent basis in the corresponding commissions. Their observers (representatives) will have the right to speak without the right to vote and will therefore not participate in the formation of a consensus. In addition each commission may invite functional governmental organizations to participate as observers ad hoc in the examination of specific questions.'

8.3. DISTRIBUTION OF RESPONSIBILITIES

Studying the distribution of the twenty-seven delegations over the four permanent commissions in which, de facto, the real business of the CIEC was done (with the exception of the very last ministerial closing stage), it becomes evident at once that the United States, Japan and the EEC were represented in all four commissions, an exceptional position which no other developing or developed country occupied in the CIEC. However, this was a meaningful and even necessary arrangement in view of the fact that what mattered was to achieve agreement on actions which were in most cases to come from the developed countries. An agreement in the commission on raw materials without the participation of, for instance, the United States, an agreement in the commission on development on, for instance, agriculture without participation by the EEC, consensus in the energy commission in the absence of Japan, these and similar examples demonstrate how much the active participation in and membership of all four commissions by the three 'big' Western economic units was needed. As a matter of fact, all members of the con-

ference naturally were <u>indirectly</u> involved in and consulted
on all matters by means of coordination procedures within the
various groups, since the final result had to be approved and
ratified with the <u>consensus</u> of <u>all</u> delegations on <u>all</u> topics.
That is also why <u>every delegation</u> had the right to attend
meetings of commissions other than its own, although only as
auditor.

Naturally those OPEC members present played a more than
average role in the CIEC, as was only to be expected at a conference which had selected energy problems as one of its main
subjects. The special position of the OPEC countries was already clearly noticeable from the number and importance of
the members of this organization who participated in the conference; this manifested itself also very conspicuously in
the distribution of the co-chairmanships, among which we find
only one non-OPEC developing country (Peru, commission on raw
materials).

On the side of the developed countries none of the commissions had a co-chairman outside the circle of the 'big three'.
This resulted in the EEC being assigned <u>two</u> co-chairmanships,
for 'development' and for 'finance', a problem which the EEC
solved by appointing one co-chairman from the circle of the
European Commission and one from the circle of the EEC Council of Ministers (in this case nominated by the country which
acted as chairman, therefore alternating every six months).
This institutional subtlety was completely in consonance with
the 'bicephalous' character of the Community delegation, as
it had, because of the dividing-up of powers and responsibilities between on the one hand the member-states and on the
other the Community as such, not <u>one</u> but <u>two</u> spokesmen: one
belonging to the Commission and one belonging to the chairmanship of the Council. Even more remarkable than the unusual-
ness of this arrangement was the relative ease with which
people both inside and outside the Community learned how to
work with and handle this construction.

Quite obvious and natural at a conference such as CIEC,
though it does not show conspicuously from the lists, was the
prominent role played at the Paris conference by countries
such as India, Pakistan and Egypt, which are densely populat-
ed but almost completely lacking in oil and other raw materials. They were particularly active in the development and
financial commissions; especially in the final negotiations
they occupied a central position with regard to crucial questions such as volume and modalities of the development aid to
be given by the industrial states, the role and resources of
the international financial establishments and questions connected with the debts of the poorest developing countries.

The developing countries had appointed <u>one</u> spokesman for
every subject or topic, who set out the point of view of the
entire group, called (in Paris) the 'Group of Nineteen'. Reference was also made to the 'Group of Eight', but the developed countries did not intend to put forward one common
point of view from the very start; up to all but the final
stage of the conference, they came forward with individual
points of view and proposals, which sometimes diverged rather
widely.

The common points of view of the 'Group of Nineteen' were
based on the resolutions which the third ministerial meeting
of the 'Group of 77' had passed in Manila in January-February,
1976 and about which it had been laid down explicitly, that
they would serve as guidelines for all members of the 'Group
of 77', in all forums, inside and outside the United Nations,
in which problems concerning trade, development and related
issues are discussed. In other words, the 'Group of Nineteen'
at the Paris dialogue had a kind of binding mandate and was
thus in a sense accountable to the 'Group of 77', with which
indeed it kept in close touch at all times.

8.4. THE PROBLEM OF CONSULTATIONS WITHIN AND BETWEEN THE GROUPS

In this connection one should keep in mind the fact that the
'Group of Nineteen' constituted, as regards their number (the
situation is totally different if one argues from population
figures, national product or similar criteria, which abstract
from the existence of sovereign states; the Group of Nineteen,
in this case, constitutes even a large majority!), only a
small minority of the well over 110 member-states of the
'Group of 77', and it had to take this fact into political
consideration. The situation of the 'Group of Nineteen' was
in this respect completely different from that of the 'Group
of Eight', which in itself already constituted the greater
part of the entire OECD group. (Of the twenty-four members
only Turkey, Greece, Austria, Norway, Finland, Portugal, Ice-
land and New Zealand were actually not present at the dialogue; moreover, these absent countries were kept informed
every day and were consulted continuously through the OECD
secretariat, which was an observer in the CIEC commissions,
and through special toplevels groups within the OECD organizations).

The process of working out and mutually attuning the positions within the groups (which is, for instance in UNCTAD,
such a laborious and protracted business that often much more
time has to be devoted to meetings within the separate groups
than to the conference proper) could be settled in Paris in
such a way that during the actual sessions every commission
was virtually in a position every day to organize either a
plenary meeting or a meeting of sub-groups or negotiating
teams.

The sessions themselves had been selected in such a way
that the industrial states in particular could choose to be
represented by officials who, in the various capitals, personally dealt with the problems in question on a responsible
level; this ruled out sessions of well over a week, since
such officials cannot possibly leave their tasks at home for
a longer period of time. Thus in the first six months of 1976
every month meetings of eight to ten days took place; work
continued during the intervening weekend. The commissions all
met in the morning or in the afternoon, while the other half
of the working day as well as the evening was set aside for
coordination within the groups and for internal activities of

the delegations.
   A representative time-table was, for instance: 8.00-9.00,
internal delegation-meetings; 9.00-10.00 (or 9.00-11.00), meetings between delegations from the two groups in final preparation of the subsequent sitting of the commission; 10.00-1.00
(or 11.00-2.00), official commission meetings, followed by a
working-lunch and informal contacts; 2.30-5.00, sectoral (i.e.,
directed towards current business and activities in one particular commission) preparation in the respective delegations
from the 'Group of Eight', followed by a meeting of the entire
'Group of Eight' on those particular topics, under the chairmanship of the co-chairman in question; after that, on some
days there were 'horizontal' meetings of the 'Group of Eight'
(that is to say, meetings which concerned themselves with the
entire range of topics of the conference) under the direction
of the Canadian co-chairmanship and with all co-chairmen at-
tending; every evening, and, at a later stage, every morning
too, 'horizontal' coordination meetings of the European Community were held. The different formations of the 'Group of
Nineteen', of course, held, mutatis mutandis, similar daily
meetings as have just been described for the 'Group of Eight'.
In addition there were frequent contacts between the co-
chairmen of the various commissions in order to arrange and
settle the organization of the discussions; it was customary
for the co-chairmen to preside by turns (for 24 hours periods)
over the sessions, while the co-chairman who was not presiding
sat next to the chair and could speak (if he so desired) to
give comments or advice on the proceedings.

8.5. THE AGENDA

The agendas of the commissions for the first six months of
1976 were fixed without much difficulty and contained virtually the complete list of items which had been brought up for
discussion in the above-mentioned 'action programme of Manila'
of the 'Group of 77', i.e., approximately all conceivable issues which are of importance in the economic North-South relations. The initial plan was that, after a thorough and exhaustive 'analytical phase' (a kind of general debate), the
conference would concentrate, in the second period of six
months, on a limited number of important, concrete points,
which might result in practical conclusions which subsequently would produce, in the ministerial final negotiations, the
results of the Paris dialogue: in this way, the second period
of six months of the CIEC would be the 'action-oriented phase'.
For that purpose, a plenary meeting in July 1976, of all twenty-seven delegations had been inserted. Senior officials dele-
gated to this meeting (in many cases other officials than those who had been active in the commissions) attempted to draw
up a kind of schedule for the final result, something which
naturally was extremely difficult, if not impossible, without
prejudging that very same result (on which negotiations had
still to take place). What also became clear on this occasion
was the fact that selection of a number of topics on which negotiations might concentrate was not feasible in practice

(which was quite understandable, because in the 'Group of 77' every topic had, as a matter of course, a number of directly interested advocates, so that the 'Nineteen' really could not stamp any topic as 'secondary', certainly not at such an early stage). The plenary meeting proceeded laboriously, therefore; it instructed the commissions to reach agreement on a working programme before the end of that very same session. This fell through on two counts: the tasks to be performed by the conference with regard to the <u>problem of debts</u> and with regard to the <u>problem of the 'purchasing power of export earnings'</u>.

Only thanks to the personal intervention by the two co-chairmen of the conference, the ministers MacEachen and Perez Guerrero, could the procedure be set in motion again; the fifth conference of heads of government and of state of the non-aligned countries (Colombo, August 1976) also played a part in this. In September, the formulae lacking for the working programme were agreed upon in Paris (in actual fact these were combinations of unilateral declarations with a partly common text) and after this the road was at long last clear for the start of real negotiations.

All parties had committed themselves to present proposals with regard to <u>all</u> items of the working programme before the end of October; this was indeed dome without delay. In October, too, a procedure for the negotiations proper was agreed upon: these were to take place in (informal) 'contact groups' made up of a small number of members of a particular commission, appointed according to topic; these 'contact-groups' worked without observers and without auditors. A few of these groups consisted of members from <u>two</u> commissions, such as, for instance, the groups for the debt problem and for international investments, because the commissions for development and for finance carried joint responsibility for those topics. Naturally this procedure (which, incidentally, worked satisfactorily) required a considerable strengthening and reinforcement of the coordination with those not-participating in the various contact groups, since the final results of the negotiations could, after all, only be approved and ratified with the consensus of all twenty-seven members participating in the conference.

The contact-groups functioned under the aegis of the co-chairmen of the commissions and reported to the plenary meetings of the commissions (sometimes to a joint meeting of two commissions; cf. the previous paragraph). The co-chairmen were also responsible for the above-mentioned reinforced coordination within the two groups.

8.6. THE RESULTS OF CIEC

Barely had the CIEC got underway in October 1976, when the whole negotiating process was postponed for five months because, before the November session, it became clear that the Government of the United States would be replaced by a new Executive in January. The intensive consultations which were going on within the Community and within the 'Group of Eight' about possible initiatives with a view to the final stage of CIEC stagnated and could in fact not be resumed intensively, with the new American Government, until March 1977. However, the problems of the North-South dialogue were to be found during those six months on the agenda of every important Western conference: the European Councils (summit conferences) at The Hague (end of 1976) and at Rome (March 1977), the bilateral meetings between the new American President and other heads of state, the Western summit in London in May 1977 (which took place in the middle of the last working session of the Paris conference) and finally the ministerial conference of the OECD shortly after the end of the CIEC, at which there were still intensive consultations about the assessment of the results and about the follow-up.

More than had ever been the case before, the ministers for foreign affairs of the industrial states were personally engaged in the negotiating process of the Paris dialogue, which was wound up with a session of four ministerial negotiating teams over and shortly after Whitsunday, 1977. This closing stage took a course which was both emotional and disillusioning; emotional because at present every North-South conference inevitably contains an emotional political component; disillusioning because in a general assessment people always look for 'success' or 'failure'. But the only adequate test of an event of this kind is the question of whether or not meaningful progress has been made. Where the whole complex of economic relations between 'North' and 'South' is at issue, there can be no question of the many problems inherent in those relations being 'solved' all at once; the Paris dialogue could for that reason be nothing more than one (relatively short) phase in a continuous process, to which the CIEC tried to give new impulses and new impetus.

Whether this will turn out to have been the case cannot be finally judged until the process has developed further in the many international forums (United Nations, UNCTAD, UNIDO, FAO-WFC, GATT, IBRD, IMF, etc.). For the time being that judgement must mainly rest in the abstract on the not insignificant texts which were approved by the ministerial conference on 2 June 1977,... but which have been given no publicity at all because, due to the extremely limited facilities of the technical secretariat of the conference, these documents were not duplicated and made available until long after the final session. In the meantime the only document published was a meaningless list of points of agreement and disagreement which did not give any decisive elucidation on the quality and the contents of these points.

No more than a brief outline of the most essential elements of the collection of texts containing the real results of the CIEC can be given here.

8.7. ASSESSMENT OF THE RESULTS

In the first place the Paris dialogue, even without being particularly innovative, has given, after all, useful, additional impulses in all kinds of areas to programmes which are already being implemented in various international bodies but which,

for whatever reason, have met with obstacles. Thus, in the
CIEC, agreement has been achieved on chapters about agriculture and about infrastructure, on many points of a chapter
about industrialization and technology, on specific monetary
programmes, on certain aspects of the energy problem. Partial
agreement has been achieved on the preferential treatment
which developing countries will receive in commercial policy
and on a number of aspects of the problem of transnational
investments. These and similar texts will certainly facilitate and accelerate discussion of the relevant problems in the
various appropriate international organizations. An example of
an issue in this category, about which no agreement was achieved, is the proposal by the 'Group of Nineteen' that the developed countries ought to refrain from every action that
would relieve the plight of industries that cannot stand up to
competition.

Some other conclusions of the CIEC, which are really of a
different order from the preceding ones, do have a certain innovative character, such as the obligation which the industrial states have undertaken to raise the volume and quality of
their development aid and to enlarge the funds of the international financial establishments (in particular, the World
Bank).

The same goes for a special $1 billion programma made avail-
able ad hoc by the participating industrial countries in aid
of specific poorer developing countries, and also, in quite a
different area, for the breakthrough as regards the formerly
so very controversial principle of a 'common fund' for the
purpose of financing commodity agreements with buffer stocks.
In addition, mention should be made of the idea (negotiations
about which were unfortunately not pursued to their conclusion) of an international inquiry with a view to the creation
of a system of stabilization of the export earnings of certain
developing countries; such a system could supplement, in a
useful fashion, the commodity agreements to be concluded with
a mechanism for price stabilization (the number of which agreements must, for technical reasons, remain limited).

In the area of the debt problem, both the 'Group of Nineteen' and the 'Group of Eight' wanted to introduce new ideas
into the negotiations; they proceeded, however, from funda-
mentally different concepts (on the one hand a general measure
for debt relief, on the other a procedure of considering each
case on its merits but via a new method and with improved criteria). The points of view of the two parties on this issue
did not come any closer to each other in Paris; positive elements of the dossier can, however, be used elsewhere in the
future.

A lot of attention has been given to the failure to achieve
agreement on a procedure for international contacts and consultations in the area of world energy problems; what people
sometimes forget is that in Paris for the first time certain
common conclusions about the energy problems were drawn by
North and South together.

It is to be hoped that when it will be clear to everybody
that consultation on world energy problems is something different from having a say in somebody else's decisions about

the price of oil, the framework for international consultations
will also come into existence. The Secretary-General of the
United Nations on his part has repeatedly emphasized the importance of the theme of worldwide cooperation on energy. It
would be a strange world in which precisely that topic which
is also of so much interest to many developing countries
would be the only one to be excluded from the international
economic dialogue. Indeed, that would definitely not be very
conducive to the development of the dialogue.

Likewise, the circumstance that no agreement was achieved in
Paris on all aspects of transnational investments (in particular on the proper procedures in case of litigation) does not
mean that negotiations on this important topic have been at
total deadlock since the middle of 1977.

In retrospect, the results of the CIEC do indeed look much
less disappointing than they appeared to the many who had
hoped, perhaps rather naively, to break most of the major
deadlocks in the North-South discussions at one stroke in the
final ministerial meeting of the Paris conference.

8.8. LATER DEVELOPMENTS

The only partially positive conclusions of the CIEC have not
led to a renewal of the confrontational atmosphere in the
North-South debate. The first test was the discussion in the
United Nations General Assembly in September 1977, about the
results of the CIEC; the second test was the first meeting of
the body set up subsequently by the General Assembly to review
further progress on the topics which the CIEC had left unsolv-
ed and which, quite naturally, were now being pursued in different UN and other forums which normally discuss and handle
such topics. Disappointment was expressed, of course, about
lack of progress on a number of items, but that could hardly
have been otherwise at meetings like these; the important
thing is that the tendency towards radicalization of the discussion which had at first characterized the period after the
oil crisis at the end of 1973 did not reappear. It seems improbable that this will still happen, after all, and should it
happen at a much later stage, there will be no link anymore
with the outcome of the CIEC. (3) That answers the first of
the alternatives which are the subject of this paper.

As to the second alternative, one cannot say either that
the CIEC has laid the foundation of a 'New International Economic Order'. The whole concept of a new international economic order is a complex matter, but it must obviously imply
sufficient leverage to improve, over a certain length of time,
the present disequilibrium in wealth and in prospects between
the different parts of the world; without this, the concept
would not make sense. Now, if one checks the texts adopted by
the United Nations in 1974 and 1975 regarding the establishment of a new international economic order and the resolutions
passed by the CIEC against this criterion, one finds many la-
cunae (in both the UN texts and in the CIEC resolutions), not
only because of reservations about or disagreements on certain

important paragraphs but also because some essential chapters
are simply lacking in the script.

For instance, no mention is made of the obligations of
groups of countries other than the industrial democracies.
But the appearance on the international scene of semi-indust-
rialized countries, with sometimes an enormous potential for
the future, makes it necessary to define the contribution they
also shall make to the improvement of the situation of the
poorer countries. The same holds true for the oil states
amongst the 'Group of 77'. In a general way the internal relations and rules of behaviour within the highly divergent and
heterogeneous membership of that group should constitute an
integral part of any new international economic order. This is
not to suggest that the better-off members of the 'Group of 77'
do not contribute to the cause; many of them do. But what is
expected of them internationally should also be made clear and
explicit in official texts.

Then there is the case of the so-called socialist countries.
They showed no inclination to participate in the Paris dialogue and their performance in the fields of aid and trade in
favour of the poor countries is minimal, a fraction of what
the industrialized democracies are doing. Apart from Bulgaria
and Roumania, which have a much lower income per capita, the
Eastern European countries and in particular the Soviet Union
are in an economic position which should, logically speaking,
put them amongst the major contributors to international development policies. A new international economic order which
fails to specify what is expected of this group of countries
is incomplete.

China is a case apart; until recently, she did not seek
active involvement in international economic relations, but
this situation seems to be changing now and could, in view of
the size and the enormous potential of the country, become a
very important new factor. (4)

8.9. PROBLEM AREAS

The case of China with her nearly one billion inhabitants illustrates the importance of demographic problems in the context of the world economic order; the resolutions about the
NIEO, however, have not taken this problem into consideration.

Problems which <u>have</u> been taken into consideration but with
an emphasis which <u>has</u> sometimes made their solution more
rather than less difficult are, for instance, those of international investments, where mutual trust and cooperation are
indispensable if a sufficiently vast transfer of resources is
to be achieved. Another example is the problem of industrial
restructuring (redeployment of industry), which is bound to
encounter strong opposition if it is felt to be envisaged without the necessary consideration for the work force affected.

In matters of trade, too much emphasis seems to have been
laid indiscriminately and without sufficient differentiation
on the raw materials sector, whereas the claim of absolute
and irrevocable preferential access for manufactured goods to
the markets of the industrialized democracies (regardless of

the relative economic strength of the individual members of
the 'Group of 77') was bound to create difficulties. On the
other hand, alternative approaches like the stabilization of
export earnings of poor countries which depend mainly on one
or two products have not received sufficient attention. The
importance of energy problems has already been underlined.

Since discussions about a new international economic order
began, the world has additionally been confronted with a pro-
longed recession and with monetary disorder. (5) Several traditional industrial sectors are going through a painful process of adjustment, investments are lagging and the danger of
protectionism is real. Drawing up blueprints for improving the
world economy and the North-South relationship certainly has
not become easier; the problems are even greater and more complex than was originally envisaged.

8.10. CONCLUDING REMARKS

The concept of dialogue rather than confrontation, however,
remains valid, not only between North and South but also within the group of industrialized democracies (and also between
East and West, to use another current simplification). The
danger of inward-looking policies being adopted because of all
kinds of very real internal pressures can be effectively coun-
tered only by continuous cooperative efforts, such as those
taking place in the GATT trade negotiations and in many other
forums.

This continuous process of international contacts and negotiations, indispensable and vital to an interdependent world,
is also essential to the relationship between the industrialized and the developing nations. Although it must be recognized that the developing nations constitute in the present
economic reality four or five groups of widely different types
of countries rather than one single group, it must also be accepted as a political fact of life that they put forward common points of view - so long as the members of the 'Group of
77' choose to do so, that is their affair. The process of negotiation may be complicated and frequently frustrating, but
there is no short cut to easy results. And this ongoing dialogue, which has been pursued in the various specialized forums since the CIEC ended, does yield tangible results from
time to time.

Thus progress is being made (although on the regional or
even bilateral rather than on the worldwide level) on some of
the more delicate aspects of the treatment of transnational
investments. Thus UNCTAD has gone into the problems relating
to raw materials in a concrete fashion, examining products one
by one rather than studying in the abstract what may be done
to eliminate excessive price fluctuations. On the vexed issue
of the 'common fund' as a policy instrument for commodities,
there is no full consensus as yet, but the gap between the
respective positions has been reduced very considerably,
thanks to and since the CIEC.

Significant progress has been made in UNCTAD on the issue
of the debts of poor countries, with the result that a case-

by-case method based on enlarged criteria is combined with special relief measures in favour of the least developed countries. (6) Again, this consensus owed much to the work previously done in the CIEC (without immediate results at the time) on these problems. It also owed much to ideas originally put forward by the European Economic Community, ideas for which the Community managed to get American and Japanese support during the CIEC. It is interesting to note in passing that the participation of the Community as such in this kind of negotiation appears to have facilitated rather than complicated the business of finding possible areas of consensus between North and South as well as within the group of OECD countries.

If the task ahead is still arduous and highly complex, there is little doubt as to the method to be followed: to utilize all opportunities for explanation and dialogue that will present themselves, in the same fashion and in the same spirit which characterized the North-South dialogue in Paris. It is a good thing that, with all the present economic difficulties, this seems now to be the prevailing mood.

FOOTNOTES

1. Articles on this subject by the present author appeared in 'Europa Archiv' 17/77 and in the 'Internationale Spectator' of September, 1977.

2. This is not the place to enter into a discussion of the shortcomings of this bipolar description of the negotiating process in question.

3. What appeared to be improbable when this paper was presented in February, 1978, has indeed not happened since then.

4. In the meantime, this change has taken spectacular proportions.

5. The present author presented, with Professor P.J.G. Kapteyn, a report on the New International Economic Order (NIEO) to the Dutch Society for International Law in September, 1977 (Kluwer, Deventer).

6. At the time this paper was read at the Department of Economics of Tilburg University, the above-mentioned progress had not yet been finalized, but it would be odd not to mention it now.

REFERENCES

Amuzegar, Jahangir, "North-South Dialogue: from Conflict to Compromise", in: Foreign Affairs, Vol. 54, April, 1976.

Amuzegar, Jahangir, "Requiem for the North-South Conference", in: Foreign Affairs, Vol. 56, October, 1977.

Burchard, Hans-Joachim, "Nord-Süd-Dialog - und wie weiter?", in: Aussen Politik, Vol. 28, pp. 393-405, 1977.

Cooper, R.N., "A New International Economic Order for Mutual Gain", in: Foreign Policy, Spring, 1977, pp. 66-120.

Friedländer, T., "Die Konferenz für internationale wirtschaftliche Zusammenarbeit [Paris, Dezember 1975 - Juni 1977] und das Dilemma des "Nord-Süd-Dialogs", in: IPW-Berichte, Vol. 6, pp. 66-70, August, 1977. Institut für internationale Politik und Wirtschaft, Berlin (D.D.R.).

"Nord-Sud: un Avenir Incertain", in: Annals of international Studies, Vol. 7 (a special issue), pp. 1-157, 1976.

"The North-South Dialogue: Success or Failure? [Discussion with Jean Durieux, Messaoud Ait Chaalal, Edmund Wellenstein]", in: The Courier: European Community-Africa, Caribbean, Pacific, September-October, 1977.

Rothstein, R.L., "Politics and Policy-making in the Third World: does a Reform Strategy make sense?", in: World Development, Vol. 4, August, 1976.

Schmidt, Rudolf, "Nord-Süd-Dialog und Weltwirtschaftsordnung", in: Aussen Politik, Vol. 28, pp. 273-284, 1977.

Schwaebel, J., "Les '77' à la Recherche d'une 'Économie Collective'", in: Mondes en Développement, No. 17, 1977.

Smyth, D.C., "The Global Economy and the Third World: Coalition or Cleavage?", (with tabulation), in: World Politics, Vol. 29, July, 1977.

Taylor, Stephen, "EEC Co-ordinator for the North-South Conference", in: The World Today, November, 1977. [appeared simultaneously in German in: Europa Archiv, Vol. 32, No. 20, 25 October, 1977]

Tardy, G., "Les Bases du Dialogue Nord-Sud: 12 Propositions", in: Chroniques d'actualité, Vol. 16, February, 1977.